S0-ABR-606

HW

to Charlie

60ᶜᶜ

ENGLISH FURNITURE

COUNTRY

C   L

LIFE

ENGLISH FURNITURE

ITS ESSENTIALS AND CHARACTERISTICS

Simply and Clearly Explained for the Student and
Small Collector

BY

JOHN C. ROGERS, A.R.I.B.A.

WITH A FOREWORD BY

H. AVRAY TIPPING, M.A., F.S.A.

LONDON

Published at the Offices of " Country Life," Ltd.,
20, Tavistock Street, Covent Garden, W.C. 2, and
by George Newnes, Ltd., 8-11, Southampton Street,
Strand, W.C. 2. New York: Charles Scribner's Sons

MCMXXIII

Printed in Great Britain

FOREWORD

By H. AVRAY TIPPING, M.A., F.S.A.

WHEN I was young few wanted to know the origin and date of the chair they sat on or of the table they wrote at. Now many do, and quite a body of literature on the subject has arisen. Surrounded by it, and yet merely needing light on some few and simple points, the amateur of old furniture feels like looking for a needle in a bundle of hay. He longs for some small yet compendious volume that will just not omit what he is likely to want to know, and not include a lot which is beyond his scope and confuses his mind.

Here he has it. By a careful and intelligent scheme of inclusion and exclusion the author gives the requisite amount and the needed kind of information, presented clearly and agreeably by the apt partnership of letter-press, photographic reproduction, and measured drawing. The reader can readily obtain a correct and comprehensive idea of when furniture, of any leading type, came into use, and of how it was altered in form and detail as time went on. He will also learn what, at various periods, was its substance, and what the mode of its construction.

All this Mr. Rogers knows about and practises. Moreover, he has shown selective acumen in choosing and marshalling his materials. Thus he has been able to combine terseness with truth, considerable technicality with perfect intelligibility. Many will find his book a helpful companion and a reliable friend.

AUTHOR'S NOTE
AND ACKNOWLEDGMENTS

THE true appreciation of works of art is the natural outcome of possessing not merely an acquaintance with, but a thorough grasp of their qualities, obvious and obscure. No one will deny that old English furniture should be included among such works. As an artistic craft it becomes, with study, an open book full of interesting details of history, fashion, and craftmanship; but those who would read this story must look a little further than the polished surface and the handsome front: every nail and dowel peg plays its modest part and forms a link in the chain of evidence by which our appreciation, and incidentally the price we may feel inclined to pay, is governed.

The history of old English furniture has been often and ably told, but very little indeed has been written concerning the practical side; yet questions of material and construction are no less valuable to the collector if he count himself a true student of his subject.

In perusing the following pages I believe the reader will appreciate the importance of this point, and thereby not only obtain a clearer comprehension of vital factors but discover also that his admiration for the old work should be based upon practical as well as æsthetic ideals.

In arranging the book I have considered it best to make three divisions or parts, which correspond with the recognised periods—in the first of which oak was chiefly used, in the second walnut, and in the third mahogany. Each part is prefaced by an historical note, followed by short chapters dealing with the development in construction and design of the various types of furniture then in use. For convenience and quick reference, the photographs are placed as near as is possible to the descriptions, and the informative underlines to each illustration are a special feature of the book; carefully prepared diagrams, explanatory of certain types and features, appear in the text, while those showing general characteristics are to be found at the end of Part III., together with a handy list of approximate dates.

In the preparation of this book, I have received much valuable assistance from the following gentlemen, who have not only placed their collections at my disposal, but have most kindly submitted to the exacting requirements of the furniture photographer:

Mr. Edward Hudson, Mr. H. Avray Tipping, Mr. Stanley J. May, Mr. Ernest Lawrence, Mr. R. Minton Taylor, Messrs. William Morris and Company, and my brother Mr. D. G. Rogers. I am also indebted to Mr. H. Avray Tipping and Mr. Ralph Edwards for reading and correcting the proofs, and to Mr. Percival D. Griffiths for particulars of specimens in his collection.

I have, moreover, to acknowledge illustrations contributed by Mr. William Harvey, Mr. Frank Partridge, Mr. R. Randall Phillips, and Messrs. Phillips of Hitchin.

JOHN C. ROGERS.

June, 1923.

CONTENTS

b

ENGLISH FURNITURE

THE PERIOD OF MAHOGANY FURNITURE

ILLUSTRATIONS

PLATES

THE PERIOD OF OAK FURNITURE

xi

ENGLISH FURNITURE

THE PERIOD OF WALNUT FURNITURE

xii

ILLUSTRATIONS

THE PERIOD OF MAHOGANY FURNITURE

ENGLISH FURNITURE

IN THE TEXT

INTRODUCTION

INTRODUCTION

In pursuing the history and characteristics of Old English furniture, the student will quickly discover that they have much in common with contemporary architecture; both of them are constructional arts of an intensely practical nature, intended primarily to supply some of the material needs of mankind.

The existence of the building gives rise to the need for furniture; and the desire to decorate and enrich the brick and masonry walls finds its counterpart in the beautiful creations in oak, walnut, and mahogany, such as are illustrated and described in this volume.

Our native furniture makes a strong appeal, not only to lovers of fine old craftsmanship here in England, but also to the colonist, and the collector and student in the States, where a singular interest arises from a comparison of the antique pieces of the old country with those taken over by the early pilgrim settlers or subsequently made there.

With the rapidly increasing difficulty in finding genuine untouched specimens many traps and pitfalls beset the collector; and if he is to escape with the minimum of blunders, his study must be ordered and guided by practical knowledge rather than capricious taste in certain directions. Firstly, there is the historical and political aspect to consider; he must know something of this in order to appreciate many a curious and perhaps sudden change in fashion, both as regards material and design.

For instance, the years of civil war and Commonwealth rule, 1640–1660, greatly checked the manufacture of all fine furniture in oak and walnut, such as was developing on traditional lines from the early Renaissance manner: very plain and rather uncomfortable pieces mark the Cromwellian régime; then, with the Restoration, came the return of the refugee noblemen from the Continent, bringing with them some furniture in veneered walnut utterly different in design and construction from the native work. A new fashion was thus suddenly introduced, and although, especially in the provinces, the popularity of oak continued under Charles II., walnut gradually increased in favour, to become supreme on the accession of William III.

Again, an invention may lead to the extinction of one type and the rise of another, as with the long-case clock, which came in suddenly owing largely to the discovery by a Dr. Hooke* of a new movement, so rendering the older brass lantern clock obsolete and unfashionable.

Secondly, there is the furniture itself, and at this stage interest should be concentrated on the three vital factors—viz., construction, form, enrichment; within these three points lie the essentials in furniture, and old work should, as a general rule, be examined in this order. It is of little use scrutinizing and feeling a piece of carving unless it be first ascertained that the member bearing it is part of the original construction, etc.

No factor can be more important than construction, and taken in conjunction with form, with which it is, of course, inseparable, it is of the greatest value as a guide to the date of a piece and as a test of its genuineness.

Many points of construction do not appear or are very obscure in photographs; consequently, I have prepared a set of diagrams which I trust will be helpful in enabling the reader to grasp quickly the many important variations and developments that occur. Changing features of design are also portrayed in this manner, and arranged in chronological order for reference and comparison.

* F. Lenygon, " Furniture in England, 1660–1760."

Form, by which mass and proportion are controlled, is again linked with the third factor, enrichment—*i.e.*, carving, inlay, painting, etc. The beautiful outline, the precise adjustment of line and curve in the old work are living testimony of the cabinet-maker's remarkable skill, and his ornament, even when profuse, was very rarely " constructed "—*i.e.*, he fully understood the golden rule that decoration, while enhancing appearance, is quite superficial and subservient to the master factors, construction and form.

It is most important that students and craftsmen of to-day should realize that all these matters which make for beauty are directly dependent upon, and arise out of, the qualities and limitations of the materials used. It is because the old craftsmen rarely exceeded these limits that their work looks right.

The amateur should at an early stage acquaint himself with the appearance and the nature of the various woods used during the succeeding periods, and with the difference between the original oiled, varnished, and waxed surfaces, and the varnished and french-polish finishes of the nineteenth and present century. He should be able to discern quickly between oak and chestnut (by no means easy with some plain cuts of oak), between walnut and mahogany (sometimes difficult when stained), also between satinwood, chestnut, and birch, and the large number of other native and foreign woods used in veneering.

The collector of experience has yet another string to his bow, in that, when contemplating the purchase of an old piece, he not only carefully examines its construction, its general lines and proportions, and the precise character and condition of the enrichment, but the surface and colour of the wood claim his special attention also.

In the case of sixteenth and seventeenth century oak, that has always been taken care of and simply polished with linseed oil or beeswax, the surface during its two and a half centuries of existence will have assumed a wonderful rich colour and fine hard polish on all easily accessible parts, a quality known as patina. This is likewise found on untouched (*i.e.*, unspoilt) walnut and mahogany, but the condition of much old furniture to-day shows indications of a hard and varied life. It is seldom, indeed, that the collector finds that glorious old polish which to the touch has something of the quality of the old lead glaze on pottery, though, if he be so fortunate, he will find it accompanied by a rather long price.

No; the vicissitudes of Old English furniture have been many: some of the oak and the major proportion of walnut and mahogany pieces were french-polished in the nineteenth century (for which process it was necessary to remove the effects of older polishing). Also during this period of vandalism many pieces, including the oak, were coated with a coarse thick varnish; some, in ignorant hands, were even painted. Then of late years, in passing through the hands of dealers, they have again been stripped, the old colour restored by stains, missing or decayed parts replaced by new or old wood, and the genuine patina faked more or less successfully by bodying up in thick shellac, rubbing down with pumice powder and oil, and then waxing.

And, worse, many pieces have been cleverly transformed into other types to sell at larger figures; in fact, no end of tricks have been played with surface, structure, and the adding of detail, etc., in the rush to make the old things meet the huge demand; and so the collector becomes a very cautious and sceptical person. But he enjoys the hunt.

There is one more point very valuable to the student, and that is the important distinction between the fashionable, costly furniture and the simpler pieces made by cabinet-makers, joiners, and even carpenters, throughout the country districts (though this distinction is much more

xxii

applicable to work after than before the Restoration). Among the former, many pieces were imported at certain periods, and those which were home-made chiefly emanated from London workshops; they one and all bear testimony to a magnificent and extravagant mode of living, both at Court and in the great houses of the nobility; and when we turn to the plain country-made furniture, we realize something of the wide gulf that existed between the " great " people of those old times and the simple-minded folk—the squires, tradesmen, and farmers of the shires—who retained in their homes the furniture of their ancestors and were perfectly contented with it generations after it had been relegated to the attic by changing fashions in the mansions of the wealthy.

Tradition died hard, and new ideas travelled slowly about conservative England; consequently, many pieces of oak furniture, richly carved, all in the early Jacobean manner, have been found bearing a date as late as 1720—*i.e.*, about one hundred years after they would have been placed had they been undated pieces. This may be rather an extreme case, but, with the exception that walnut and mahogany were not dated, it applies to all periods of design; and even when country examples are not unduly late, they are often feeble copies of the London pieces. Generally native oak was substituted, for reasons of transport and expense, for the fashionable walnut veneers or Spanish mahogany.

All this often presents a great problem to those who would solve the age riddle of many a simple yet very pleasing piece.

The country furniture of cottage and farm-house type include many articles — such as dressers, Windsor and rush-seated chairs—that never appeared among the fine and elegant appointments of stately rooms.

There exists, therefore, in Old English furniture a pretty faithful record of all classes of the community for the last four hundred years; also, with many of their old homes still in a good state of preservation, it is possible to construct at least a mental picture of the way in which our ancestors lived and went about their work—that handiwork in which can be traced the pleasure it must have given those simple folk who produced it—much of it plain and even rough, " yet in such sweet accord with the familiar nature amidst which they dwelt that, when by some happy chance we come across the work they wrought, untouched by any but natural change, it fills us with a satisfying, untroubled happiness that few things else could bring us. . . . Call this sentiment if you please, but you *know* that it is true " (William Morris).

Part I

THE PERIOD OF OAK FURNITURE
(*Circa* 1450–1685)

A

I.—HISTORICAL NOTE

UNLIKE the succeeding periods in furniture design, it is little short of impossible to give a date at which the age of oak commenced, but we know that it was a truly English style, developing and changing with the great tradition in Gothic building. Of the very early work— that corresponding with the " Early English " and " Decorated " periods in Gothic architecture (viz., 1200– 1280 and 1280–1370)—there is hardly a stick of domestic furniture left, but in many of our cathedrals and parish churches chests, etc., remain, in addition to fixed furniture, such as screens and benches, which give a good idea of early mediæval woodwork.

The Black Death, 1348–1350, marks the dividing line; this terrible scourge swept away half the population of England, put a very severe check upon all crafts, and when it had passed the country was in a dilemma. The majority of the skilled men of experience had died, taking with them the old traditions and methods of working. With labour scarce, none too skilled, and extremely expensive, the rich and lavish " Decorated " Gothic could not long endure; consequently, by 1370–1380 new methods were being evolved, to be fully developed as the " Perpendicular " style, which reached its culmination under the first Tudor king.

It is therefore at a date approximately one hundred years after the Black Death that an outline study of English furniture may appropriately commence.

During the fifteenth century domestic furniture was scarce, restricted to absolute necessities, and for the most

3

part crudely made by carpenters, but with the opening of the sixteenth century greater skill and refinement were in evidence.

Construction was of the simplest, though sound and efficient, and where ornament was worked it took the form of low relief, or pierced patterns of tracery, or formal foliage, such as were in fashion at the time with the stone-masons.

But the most important means of decoration at this period was colour; unfortunately, the merest fragments remain on furniture, but many chancel screens survive with their original scheme of bright reds, blues, greens, and gilt applied over carved enrichment and in portraying figure subjects; and this evidence is supported by the limner's work on ancient manuscripts, etc., wherein the few and plain pieces of furniture are shown decorated in strong colours.

The whole surface of the wood was generally lime-whitened, to be followed by a polychromatic scheme of decoration carried out in oil colour or in tempera—*i.e.*, earth and mineral pigments and vegetable dyes mixed with yolk of eggs, honey, and sometimes with wax.

About the middle of the sixteenth century new ideas and practices were introduced: the painting of furniture was going out, though carved decoration remained in vogue, the surface of the oak being sometimes left in its natural state; in other cases, at time of manufacture poppy or linseed oil, often dyed with alkanet root, was rubbed in, and in the seventeenth century beeswax with turpentine was constantly used in polishing and reno-vating the surfaces, the primary object being to preserve the wood.

Furniture of the sixteenth century was far from plentiful, and such as has survived was mostly made for wealthy patrons.

Wonder-buildings like Hampton Court and Nonesuch

were furnished to the last degree of extravagance, but they did not represent the typical house up and down the country, where local-made furniture would chiefly be employed, and only in sufficient quantity for the practical needs of the household.

The yeoman can have possessed very little: a cumbersome table and a few chairs, stools, or benches, a bread hutch, some kind of low bed, possibly a cradle, all of a very plain and massive type, such as had been passed on for many generations and remained throughout in the same building.

The reign of Elizabeth was remarkable for a distinct advance in many directions. It was an era of great building activity; such famous old mansions as Wollaton, Montacute, Kirby, and Longleat being built between 1570 and 1585, on most of which some Italian craftsmen were probably employed, and the names of John Thorpe, R. Smythson, and others are mentioned as architects, denoting their position as a distinct entity in the art of building. This point is important, for it marks the beginning of the architect's influence, to be traced with growing intensity through the seventeenth and eighteenth centuries, until, as noted later, not only the house, but all its furniture and appointments, were sometimes designed by him and executed under his direction.

In these great houses (still standing in fine preservation to-day, with the exception of Kirby Hall) the planning was more complex than in the earlier feudal type. Measures of defence were discarded, each room had its fireplace, and the walls of the principal rooms were panelled in wainscot to a height of about 8 to 10 feet.

Much beautiful work was expended on this panelling, and special features, embodying rich carving, were the great staircases, and the remarkable fireplaces in the hall, state rooms, long gallery, etc. The detail is characterized by a quaint rendering of classic motifs, often blended with

5

Gothic forms, which still came instinctively to the hand of the country joiner and mason.

Elizabethan furniture is very rich in carving of a similar type, figure subjects in bold relief being very popular, and inlay or marquetry in wood, bone, and ivory was also in fashion, being another introduction from Italy. This marquetry was let into the solid, and is to be found on fine pieces made in oak or in walnut.

During the reign of James I. there was a slow development of furniture design, chiefly influenced by the increasing classicism of architecture with ever-growing divergence from Gothic picturesqueness. The great architect, Inigo Jones, was practising between 1614 and the early years of the Civil War, his Palladian buildings having no small effect on all forms of dependent art.

Towards the end of this reign there was a distinct diminution in bold carving, so characteristic of the true Elizabethan pieces, and a tendency to purer profile of mouldings and their use in more important form around panels, on cornices, etc., though in this respect the cabinet-makers were some years behind the joiners who made the wainscot for rooms.

Charles I. was a discerning patron of the arts, and his collection would be the treasured possession of the nation to-day, but for the Civil War and Cromwell's disposal of the contents of the numerous palaces. This act is significant of the Puritan conscience, and largely explains their preference for plain and seemingly uncomfortable pieces, giving the impression that they were made only for the essential needs of the house. Production must have been very limited during the actual years of open warfare, but about 1650 there appeared a decided impetus in furniture making, many good cupboards, settles, etc., being of about this date, and the very plain Cromwellian turning on chair legs, etc., was becoming more interesting and thoughtful. Many seats and backs were stuffed and covered with stamped and coloured leathers, the idea, and very often the material, being imported from the Continent.

By the year 1655 the country was tired of war and the Protector's methods; feeling was growing in favour of a restored monarchy, and public taste generally was improving.

The inevitable culmination was the return to England in 1660 of Charles II., coupled with an ardent desire all over the country for a freer and gayer life. This was immediately reflected in furniture, which came into its own again as a craft upon which much skill and artistic effort were expended.

This revival, however, marks the last few years of the great period of oak. The restored king and the returned refugee noblemen had learnt much on the Continent, and were bringing back with them pieces of walnut furniture, and inducing Dutch and French craftsmen to enter their service in this country; consequently, there is a certain amount of French, Italian, and Dutch feeling in the oak pieces made for the remainder of the seventeenth century, such as ebony appliqué and inlay with ivory, mother of pearl, etc., and the sparing use of Eastern woods in similar form. Such furniture was made and used contemporaneously with the work in solid walnut, such as chairs, stools and day-beds, in which the characteristic motif is the twist turning which first appeared about the time of the Restoration.

Before passing on to consider the various types of oak furniture, it is very important to understand something of the wood itself. English oak is the most durable of all growths, but it is also the most tricky to work, and there is no doubt as to the importance which the old-time craftsmen attached to the seasoning processes, a vital point in ensuring that their work would " hold up " and remain sound.

The trees being of ripe old age (about 200 years), and

having been felled and barked at the right seasons, the logs were immersed in a running stream,* after which, having been allowed to dry out, they were taken to the sawpits† and converted into planks, boards, and beams.

The two-handed saw worked almost vertically, operated by two men, one above and the other below the log, called top and bottom sawyer, and the pair always kept together, as it was essential to know each other's stroke and throw.

Next ensued a long period of several years during which the planks were lying in the open, but above ground, and kept apart to allow the complete circulation of air; in this way the oak became thoroughly dry and mellow, but however long the process, when it came to being worked up on the bench—a new surface exposed by saw or plane— the effect of the atmosphere would cause it to move again, and for this reason there was no attempt to hurry the work. In fact, it was the tradition to pass from one job to another in the workshop, so allowing the work to take up its final " set " before tightening up the tenons and securing with the oak dowel pegs; in this period glue was little used.

To revert to the sawyer's work of conversion: there are two methods which have always been employed. One utilizes almost every square inch of the log, and the other is wasteful of a certain amount; but judging by the old oak furniture remaining, it was more often adopted. By

* Immersion varied from four or six weeks to several years, according to type of growth.

† It appears that little oak was converted by saw prior to the latter part of the sixteenth century, the mediæval method having been the employment of the beetle and wedge, by which scantlings were skilfully split from the log, it being known that split timber is more easily seasoned. To this day the roofs of many old buildings retain their original rafters of split oak. In finishing split oak for furniture the surfaces were trimmed with the adze, the marks of which are easily discernible on many pieces, especially on the backs of panels.

8

the first method the tree was sawn down in parallel planks, which would gradually diminish in width on each side from the central plank; the result is that, with the exception of a few central boards, the *edges* reveal the beautiful silver grain where it can have no value, the broad surfaces showing very plain and uninteresting grain. By the second method the opposite result is obtained, providing figured oak on every board. The tree is first quartered in the direction of its length, then each triangular quarter is sawn into planks by cuts that practically follow the radiating lines known as medullary rays, which are actually the silver grain or figure.

The boards so produced would not be so wide as those obtained by the first method, but their general use is to be attributed to their greatly superior hardness, durability, and little tendency to warp; the silver grain, being practically free from cellular structure, reduces shrinkage to a minimum.

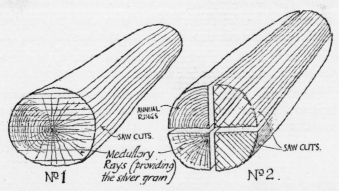

No. 1.—Tree trunk showing most economical cutting, which in oak
   does not reveal the silver grain (except at the diameter).

No. 2.—Tree trunk " quartered," showing one method of cutting
   oak to obtain figured surfaces, which is still done by
   hand at the sawpit.

II.—CHESTS

EVERY household of mediæval England probably possessed an oaken chest; it was an essential piece of furniture, serving both as a commodious and safe storage and also as a seat.

The majority of Gothic chests were of massive plank construction. Of the very early type, that at Stoke D'Abernon Church, Surrey, is a good example, dating from the thirteenth century. This chest has front and back, each formed of three planks, the central one placed horizontally and butting upon the other two, which are arranged vertically and are carried lower to form feet; the ends are cross-braced over a solid board.

This type appears to have continued until well into the fifteenth century, though there were many variations in which the construction was masked by architectural features, such as buttresses and applied tracery, and the width of the stiles greatly decreased.

Towards the close of the fifteenth century a simple chest was evolved in which the sides were carried lower than front and back to form feet, the members being united by iron straps and, or by, stout hand-wrought iron nails or oak dowel pegs.

The top was attached generally with wrought-iron strap hinges, also secured with nails, but in some cases, in place of hinges, iron wire staples linked together formed a rough sort of hinge. In the sixteenth and seventeenth centuries this type of chest became modified. Reduced in size and made of six thin boards ($\frac{5}{8}$ to $\frac{3}{4}$ inch), it continued in use for many years after panelled construction was adopted (Fig. 1).

CHEST CONSTRUCTION

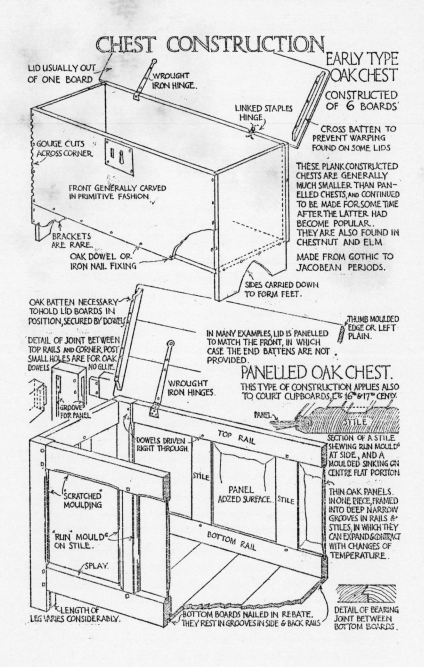

EARLY TYPE OAK CHEST

CONSTRUCTED OF 6 BOARDS

LID USUALLY OUT OF ONE BOARD

WROUGHT IRON HINGE.

LINKED STAPLES HINGE

CROSS BATTEN TO PREVENT WARPING FOUND ON SOME LIDS

GOUGE CUTS ACROSS CORNER

FRONT GENERALLY CARVED IN PRIMITIVE FASHION

THESE PLANK CONSTRUCTED CHESTS ARE GENERALLY MUCH SMALLER THAN PANELLED CHESTS, AND CONTINUED TO BE MADE FOR SOME TIME AFTER THE LATTER HAD BECOME POPULAR. THEY ARE ALSO FOUND IN CHESTNUT AND ELM

MADE FROM GOTHIC TO JACOBEAN PERIODS.

BRACKETS ARE RARE.

OAK DOWEL OR IRON NAIL FIXING

SIDES CARRIED DOWN TO FORM FEET.

OAK BATTEN NECESSARY TO HOLD LID BOARDS IN POSITION, SECURED BY DOWEL

THUMB MOULDED EDGE OR LEFT PLAIN.

DETAIL OF JOINT BETWEEN TOP RAILS AND CORNER POST SMALL HOLES ARE FOR OAK DOWELS   NO GLUE.

GROOVE FOR PANEL

IN MANY EXAMPLES, LID IS PANELLED TO MATCH THE FRONT, IN WHICH CASE THE END BATTENS ARE NOT PROVIDED.

WROUGHT IRON HINGES.

PANELLED OAK CHEST.

THIS TYPE OF CONSTRUCTION APPLIES ALSO TO COURT CUPBOARDS, ETC 16TH & 17TH CENTY.

PANEL   STILE

SECTION OF A STILE SHEWING RUN MOULDG AT SIDE, AND A MOULDED SINKING ON CENTRE FLAT PORTION

DOWELS DRIVEN RIGHT THROUGH.

TOP RAIL

STILE

PANEL ADZED SURFACE.   STILE

"SCRATCHED" MOULDING

THIN OAK PANELS. IN ONE PIECE, FRAMED INTO DEEP NARROW GROOVES IN RAILS & STILES, IN WHICH THEY CAN EXPAND & CONTRACT WITH CHANGES OF TEMPERATURE.

"RUN" MOULD ON STILE.

BOTTOM RAIL

SPLAY.

LENGTH OF LEG VARIES CONSIDERABLY.

BOTTOM BOARDS NAILED IN REBATE. THEY REST IN GROOVES IN SIDE & BACK RAILS

DETAIL OF BEARING JOINT BETWEEN BOTTOM BOARDS.

11

Iron locks were invariably fitted—let in from the external face—a hinged staple being fixed on the inside of the lid, which, when the latter was shut, entered the lock by a hole in the face-plate; the staple, when free, also serving as a handle with which to lift the lid.

These small plank chests were in some cases plain, but more often were enriched with slight mouldings and low relief carving. Besides oak, chestnut wood and elm were used, but very few have survived.

At the beginning of the sixteenth century panelling, as used on the walls, was being adopted as the principle of furniture construction. Panelled chests are now rare prior to Elizabeth, but became very general in the last quarter of the sixteenth century. They represent good sound joinery as compared with the earlier, crude carpentry productions. The diagram on page 11 clearly shows how they were framed up; the panels are each of one thin piece, and all joints connecting the rails and stiles are the mortice and tenon, assembled without glue, and secured with one or two dowel pegs cut square and driven through from face to face in circular bored holes.

One of the most important characteristics of oak period framing is the flush surface on the outer faces of all joints, such as junctions of stiles with rails, and under-framing and stretchers with the legs; this came about as a structural necessity, due to the pegs being placed very close to the edge of the mortised member. When the pegs were driven into the holes, it would have caused the wood to split had not the shoulder of the tenon been flush and tight up to the edge to prevent it. This detail became such a fast tradition that we find it still in use in the later eighteenth-century mahogany fashions, long after the reason for its use had ceased to exist.

These chests were often of considerable size, and the lid was either formed of two or three boards (Fig. 2), or was panelled to match the front (Fig. 3). When of the former

FIG. I.—A SMALL OAK CHEST ILLUSTRATING THE EARLY TYPE OF PLANK CONSTRUCTION ADOPTED FOR THOSE OF SMALL DIMENSIONS DURING THE SIXTEENTH AND SEVEN-TEENTH CENTURIES.

Judging by the crudely carved front this specimen dates from the end of the sixteenth century.
Its five planks are held together by oak dowels. The top swings on staple hinges and the
typical gouge-cut corners are here in evidence.

Length, 3 ft. 2 in.   Height, 1 ft. 9 in.   Depth, 1 ft. 1 in.

The property of Stanley J. May, Esq.

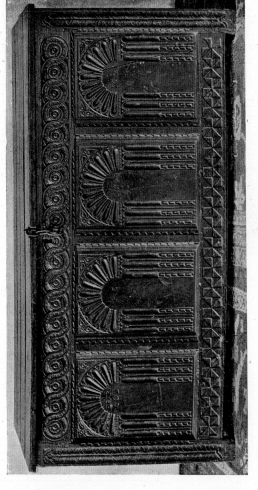

FIG. 2.—A LARGE OAK CHEST, DATED 1594.

The Renaissance influence is apparent in the guilloche ornament of the top rail and in the arcaded treatment of the carved panels.

The lid is formed of four boards secured by cross-battens.

FIG. 3.—AN OAK CHEST INSCRIBED "W R 1643."

The usual type, with three panels on front and back and two at the sides. The lid is also panelled. Observe the small scratched mouldings dying out at the junctions and the broader "run" moulds on the sides of the intermediate stiles.

The carving is of two sorts—in relief and incised. The initials and date are filled with black wax composition. Side panels, carved, became common in the seventeenth century.

Width, 3 ft. 9 in. Depth, 1 ft. 8 in. Height, 2 ft. 2 in.

The property of Stanley J. May, Esq.

FIG. 4.—AN OAK CHEST OF DRAWERS (MID-SEVENTEENTH CENTURY).

This chest is a late example of the period 1625–50, during which it was the practice to enclose the lower drawers with a pair of doors. The drawers retain the early type of grooved runners in the sides. The split-applied mouldings and handles are lacquered black to simulate ebony. The central raised panels and the radiating rails are faced with a close-grain wood resembling pear or cherry tree.

Height, 3 ft. 9 in.   Width, 3 ft. 4 in.   Depth, 1 ft. 10 in.

The property of Stanley J. May, Esq.

type, the lid boards were held in position by a cross-bearer placed transversely on the under side at the ends and fixed with several dowel pegs; when shut, these bearers appeared outside the chest.

Another type of bearer was fixed across the end edges of the lid boards, also pegged on. The hinges were generally of the type shown in the diagram.

A small box with its own lid was often framed in at one end near the top, 4 to 6 inches wide, and the full depth of the chest, entailing the use of three extra pieces, one of which was the lid, hinging on small round projections which fitted into corresponding holes in the chest framing. The side and bottom were housed in grooves, so avoiding all nailing, and necessitating the fitting in of the box while the chest itself was being assembled.

Enrichment varied between simple mouldings on the framing surrounding the panels to rich but rather coarsely executed carving, often covering the entire surfaces of framing and panels of the front, the sides being less ornate, and the back panels, though moulded, were not carved. A favourite type was the arcaded panel, the arch being built up or carved on the panel (Fig. 2); also a series of arches, flutes, lunettes, or interlacing circles on the framing (Figs. 2 and 3). Types of arabesque or strap-work patterns, gouge cuts, and many other simple devices of direct tool work trick out the surface.

A " reserve " was sometimes left in the centre of a band of ornament, in which were carved initials, or name, and a date.

The carving was treated in two ways, the best pieces being worked in relief, and cheaper productions being merely incised, as Fig. 1.

The mouldings surrounding the panels are important. On many examples they consist of two types, the first being the " scratched " mould, which is not continuous, but " dies out " on the surface, to leave a plain, square edge

13

where the uprights butt against the rails. It is to be found in most cases along the bottom edge of the top rail, and also on the inner edges of the corner posts, as Fig. 3.

The second is a moulding of more comely profile, run continuously on both edges of the intermediate uprights, or stiles; it is cut off square to butt against the top rail, and at the bottom the moulded stile is cut back on the splay to accord with the splayed top edge of the bottom rail, a curious feature which always obtained, and suggests the " weathering " of a cill (Fig. 3).

This splay, which is also termed a " chamfer," is on some chests found stopped with a moulded finish in Gothic manner on either side of the junction with each stile, instead of the ordinary continuous splay. A good example may be seen on a seventeenth-century chest at the Geffery Museum, Shoreditch.

In all cases these mouldings are part of the member on which they appear.

Chests of Elizabethan character continued to be made throughout the seventeenth century in country districts, but there were distinct changes in decoration and construction appearing during James I.'s reign. The sides and backs were panelled, joinery was improving, and the construction much less solid.

The crude, scratched mould was often replaced by the continuous "run" variety, in most cases still part of the solid framing, and we note an advance in skill by their being mitred at the corners, though during the previous century beautifully mitred mouldings were placed around panels on important cupboards, etc., and it is also found on wall panelling of that date. The splay on the top edge of bottom rail was still often used, and an important moulding planted on around the base just above the feet (Fig. 4).

Floral and pattern carving are met with, but the infinite variety and inventiveness of the carvers' work was giving way to a regular use of stock ornament, which consisted of

14

monotonous repeats carved on long strips and cut off to suit the dimensions of the piece under construction without regard to the spacing of the pattern. The more characteristic chests were enriched with formal raised forms on the panels with splayed lozenge shapes, and split, turned pieces glued on, chiefly on stiles and rails (Fig. 4).

The arch in the panel again appears, but more closely resembles its constructional contemporary in masonry. Low relief strap work was also general, and is often found on the Bible boxes which were made in great numbers at this period and through the Commonwealth, their construction being similar to the small type of plank chests.

The lids of the large chests were generally panelled, and the edge had a definite thumb mould.

These types of chest decoration continued into Charles I.'s reign, the beauty and delightful invention of Gothic carving being by this time a thing of the past; and, regarding the mouldings, as a general rule they were much shallower, and certainly less interesting than the Elizabethan mouldings.

Much play was made of mitreing the mouldings in and out around the panels, and this necessitated their being run on separate strips of oak, to be very accurately fitted and glued and bradded in position (Fig. 4). Chests of this type were made for the remainder of the seventeenth century and well into the eighteenth, but with the passing of the Stuarts were of country origin, as the chest formed no part of the scheme of furnishing in walnut.

The " mule chest," or dower chest, with its proverbial bottom drawer, is an interesting transition between the box-type chest and the chest of drawers. They first appeared about 1590, and were made with one or two drawers placed beneath the box portion; the drawers had stout sides, which were grooved to slide on the early form of runner, and rough dovetailing was attempted; the bottom boards were placed transversely and fixed with nails.

15

III.—CHESTS OF DRAWERS

THE complete chest of drawers quickly developed from the mule chest, and by about 1660 appears to have been made in fairly large numbers. Mouldings were planted on the carcase framing and on the drawer fronts to give panel effects in several rectangular designs, entailing many mitres of various angles and accurate fitting. A favourite treatment was to form two distinct panels on the face of one drawer, so giving the effect of a couple, though the deception is never complete on account of the central keyhole (Fig. 4). During the second quarter of the seventeenth century a type of sub-cornice divided the chest a little above half its height, and below this projection a pair of finely panelled doors were hung to enclose three or four drawers (Fig. 4). About 1660 the doors were omitted, and for the remainder of the century all drawers were exposed, as in the walnut designs.

On the side panelling, the frieze, and the drawer fronts, split turned bobbins and egg shapes were often applied; they were frequently lacquered black to simulate ebony (Fig. 4).

The corner posts or stiles of the frame were carried down as supports, but frequently the latter were bun-shaped or bracket feet, and occasionally a separate stand consisting of shallow arches with five or six stumpy turned legs.

About 1690 the stand increased in height, one or two drawers being included in its framing, and the legs—four, five, or six—were baluster turned and united by shaped or turned stretchers after the manner of contemporary walnut examples.

16

The dovetailing of the drawers was much improved, and they ran on side strips, forming part of the horizontal divisions between the drawers, the bottom boards being no longer transverse, but fixed front to back and nailed. Wooden knobs—turned, shaped, or carved—were general for drawer pulls (Figs. 4 and 6), but brass drops, as used on the walnut pieces, were also often used.

IV.—CUPBOARDS—AUMBRIES

In the larger households the possession of one or more standing cupboards dates from very early times. But it is not until the fifteenth century that we find any mention of a livery cupboard. The name is spelt variously—liverei, lyvere, etc. It was until *circa* 1550 a cup-board—*i.e.*, without doors, from which liveries of food and drink were served out to the household, the allowance to retainers.

*1483. Liber Niger, etc.—" Taking every of them for his Livery at night, half a chet loaf, one quart of wine, one gallon of ale; and for winter livery, from All Hallowtide till Easter, one percher wax,† one candle wax."

From about 1550 the livery cup-board began to be enclosed, and the old method of piercing the panels with tracery was utilized to ventilate the interior, the piercings taking the form of geometrical cutting and moulding on the lines of contemporary window tracery (Fig. 5).

A smaller type was the hanging cupboard, in which the front was largely composed of turned balusters, of which good examples are to be seen at Victoria and Albert Museum and at St. Albans Abbey.

The doors were generally hung on wrought-iron hinges, sometimes of elaborate smith's work, and were secured with oak turn-buckles and locks.

No doubt many of these cupboards were originally painted in tempera or oil colour.

* The New Oxford Dictionary.
† A candle for placing on a perch.

FIG. 5.—A STANDING CUPBOARD IN OAK (*c.* 1500).

Framed up with moulded rails and stiles, the front panels are pierced with Gothic designs and tracery. The latter is of the contemporary perpendicular sort.

Height, 5 ft. 4½ in.   Width, 4 ft. 2 in.

Victoria and Albert Museum.

FIG. 6.—AN OAK CUPBOARD WITH DRAWERS IN FRIEZE
(SEVENTEENTH CENTURY).

Probably made in the reign of Charles I. or during the Commonwealth.

This piece exhibits Continental influence, particularly in the effect of a vaulted corridor in perspective forming the central feature of the panels, which is a motif derived from Italian work. The hollow-cut brackets on the frieze and the applied pilaster strips savour of Flemish origin.

The later (Tudor) cupboards were panelled on the same principle as the chests; and during the sixteenth century the original purpose of the livery cupboard was declining, tending to become a store for plate and other articles in use on the table.

The Gothic aumbry was a cupboard enclosed by doors, and, like the chest, was generally of simple plank construction, with one or two doors, and containing shelves, which were held in position and made part of the structure by " housing " the ends and fixing with oak dowel pegs driven through the vertical sides into them, until panelled framing was adopted in the sixteenth century.

V.—BUFFETS

THESE pieces were similar to the cup-board, and were in general use during the second half of the sixteenth century and until the Restoration. They consisted, in their simplest form, of three large shelves for the display of plate and prepared dishes, being supported at the two back corners by flat posts, and at the front corners by two tiers of richly carved bulbous columns (Fig. 7). Other specimens of the sixteenth and seventeenth centuries had the space between the top and middle shelves enclosed with panels and doors, the front being flat. By 1610 the columns were giving place to baluster turned supports of smaller diameter.

The shelves were moulded on edge and only about $\frac{1}{2}$ inch thick, being held down by oak dowels.

Under the two upper shelves a carved frieze was usually formed, in the lower of which (*i.e.*, the middle shelf) it was general to form a drawer on grooved runners (Fig. 7).

In some late examples the cupboard between the top and middle shelves had canted sides, always panelled and generally carved. Inlay of other woods was also a feature, and many were dated.

Soon after the Restoration they went out of fashion, the long side table being retained in preference, but frequently in the latter, drawers and cupboards were formed in the space beneath the top.

FIG. 7.—A CUP-BOARD OR BUFFET OF WALNUT TREE (*c*. 1590).

The majority were made in oak but many fine specimens of furniture were in walnut at this period, constructed and formed like the oak pieces.

The enrichment is composed of elaborate carving and geometrical marquetry, the central shelf being also inlaid.

There are two drawers, one under the top shelf (with marquetry front) and the other under the centre shelf, which is almost disguised by the continuous arabesque carving in relief. Both drawers have grooved sides for runners, their sides and bottom boards being of oak.

Width, 4 ft.   Depth, 1 ft. 6 in.   Height, 3 ft. 11 in.

Victoria and Albert Museum.

FIG. 8.—AN OAK COURT CUPBOARD DATED 1610.

Typical of the shape of Elizabethan and Early Jacobean specimens, having a spacious lower cupboard enclosed with a pair of panelled doors, and surmounted by a pair of shallower cupboards, providing space for an open shelf upon which the large bulbous supports stand and, in appearance, support the projecting cornice. Very typical of good specimens is the arched central panel (enriched with the guilloche) and the flanking pilasters, which in this instance have strong Continental feeling.

The frieze of the cornice is finely carved with alternating square and circular "strap-work," the former filled with a sort of star flower and the latter with rosettes.

The gadrooning of the bulbous supports is a favourite motif. The geometrical patterns on the upper panels, with border strips on the doors, are interesting though simple examples of early "cut-in" marquetry.

The dowel pegs, which can be distinctly seen at the joints of the framing of the lower doors, should be carefully noted, their position—i.e., the distance between each pair—is conclusive proof that the panel moulds were run on the solid, otherwise the widths of the tenons could not have been greater than the plain (middle) parts of rails and muntins, in which case the pegs would show closer together.

The hinges are not original and much too big, they are of a type used throughout the seventeenth century on internal doors to unimportant rooms and shutters.

Width, 5 ft.   Depth, 2 ft. 1 in.   Height, 5 ft. 4 in.

Victoria and Albert Museum.

VI.—COURT CUPBOARDS

THE court cupboards are of box formation, like contemporary chests, being panelled on all sides and carved in a similar manner. They were a repetition of the buffet, with the lower part also enclosed.

They were in general use in large establishments for about one hundred and ten years from *circa* 1550, though country examples are found of post-Restoration date. The lower part was fitted with shelves and faced with doors, over which came a thin table top, and above this rose a short and shallower cupboard topped with a bold cornice (Fig. 8).

At the two front corners a stumpy bulbous column was usually placed, which in the sixteenth-century examples was frequently carved with crude acanthus leaf and capped with weird Ionic volutes, etc. About 1620 the column supports appear uncarved, and turned in squat baluster and vase forms. In Charles I.'s reign the columns tend to disappear entirely, and as a reminder of their former use turned knobs depend from the cornice.

The top cupboard had splayed sides in some cases, so allowing more room for display. The large lower doors appear to have had iron hinges in all cases, but the small upper doors frequently swung on oak dowels, fixed vertically between top and bottom rails of the door and framing, while the whole piece was being assembled.

The wrought-iron hinges on late sixteenth-century and the seventeenth-century examples were kept small, though still showing on the face. They interfered very little with

21

the moulded and carved stiles and posts, and their most usual form was a wedge or butterfly shape, being narrowest on the knuckle. They were always secured with iron nails. Other types of hinge used were the ornamental " cockspur " and the H, though the latter are rarely original (Fig. 29).

This method of hinging the doors was altered on many of the cabinet chests of the Commonwealth and Charles II. periods, in which the doors extend to the *full width* of the piece, so that the hinges show only when the doors are opened, and are very similar in shape to our modern " butt " hinge, though hand-made and *not* countersunk for screws.

In country districts, particularly in the north, the court cupboard was made until the opening of the eighteenth century, and on similar lines to examples one hundred years earlier.

VII.—TABLES, STOOLS, AND FORMS

THE earliest type of English table appears to have been of trestle construction—*i.e.*, the under-framing consisted of two solid, shaped ends secured to massive feet, and held rigidly in position by one or two stretcher beams; the latter were tusk-tenoned through the trestles, being " pulled up " tight by oak wedges passing through holes in the tusks. In this way they could be dismantled and reassembled with ease.

The top consisted of three or four massive planks with cross-battens on the under side, which registered its position on the top of the trestles.

About the middle of the sixteenth century the draw table came into use, and soon superseded the earlier type, having the convenience of being capable of extension to almost double length by pulling out a pair of under leaves, and all self-contained. The diagrams on page 25 explain the mechanism of this interesting table. Large turned legs were placed at the four corners, which in the Elizabethan examples were richly carved (Figs. 9 and 10). The main under frame tenoned into the tops of the legs (left square above the enrichment), and bulky connecting stretcher rails were provided just above ground level.

The main under-framing provided a frieze for decoration, which on fine examples was carved or inlaid on all sides (Figs. 9, 10 and 11).

Stretchers had two phases, the earlier type having a flat member fixed along the top surface and projecting on each side, so making it T-shaped in section (Fig. 9). But about the commencement of the seventeenth century this

23

appears to have given place to the normal rectangular section, often slightly moulded (Fig. 10).

Very long dining tables with single fixed top were often made for great establishments, having six or eight legs, but the width seldom exceeded 3 feet (Fig. 11). Side tables on four or six legs, but similar in design, also did duty in the hall, and owing to their place against a wall the frieze was only carved on the front.

The type of carving on the legs and framing was similar to that on contemporary court cupboards and chests.

The table tops were formed of massive planks with cross-framed ends, and when not designed as draw tables were held in position by under battens, or by a number of oak dowels driven down into the under-framing.

The first quarter of the seventeenth century saw little change in these heavy oak dining and side tables, though carving was gradually diminishing, the legs being turned and moulded. The draw table, however, appears to have gone out of fashion by the accession of Charles I.

About 1625 another, and much smaller, type of oak table was in general use. Its construction was light, and when designed as a side table it had one or two drawers in the frieze. These drawers were arranged directly under the top, there being no locking rail in the frieze or under-framing (Fig. 12), in contrast with the eighteenth-century types, and prior to 1660 the sides were grooved for runners.

The legs were out of 2 by 2 inch oak turned in prevailing fashions in baluster, ball, reel, and knob forms. Left square where the stretchers tenoned into them, the legs were again turned into a type of vase-shaped foot. Such tables were designed for writing, cards, or as dressing tables.

The tops, which measured about 3 feet wide by 2 feet deep, were always thin, about $\frac{5}{8}$ inch, with thumb moulded edges and dowelled down to the framing.

Many slight variations occur, but in the main they

FIG. 9.—A DRAW TABLE, POSSESSING EXCEPTIONALLY WELL CARVED AND PROPORTIONED LEGS WITH
SHAPED BASE BLOCKS (c. 1580).

*Two woods are here used in conjunction: the top with draw leaves and the underframe are oak, the latter having applied mouldings in
carved pine. The carved bulbous legs are in pine. The stretchers—of* **T** *section—have the flat top member in pine while the rectangular
portion is in oak.*

[Height, 2 ft. 11½ in.   Breadth of top, 3 ft. 1½ in.   Length, 9 ft. 0½ in.

The property of the Marquis Curzon.]

FIG. 10.—A FINE SPECIMEN OF AN OAK DRAW TABLE (*c.* 1600).

The bulbous turned legs are carved with the acanthus and have Ionic caps. The main underframe has a richly inlaid frieze on all sides.

[Length, 5 ft. 11 in.   Width, 2 ft. 9 in.   Height, 2 ft. 9 in.   Extended top, 11 ft.

Victoria and Albert Museum.]

FIG. 11.—A LONG DINING OR BANQUETING TABLE IN OAK (c. 1600–10).

The top is composed of massive planks, in one length, cross-framed at the ends. The main underframe has a carved fluted frieze and the legs are very bulky and moulded on the lathe.

Such a table would probably be assembled in the room or hall, as it would be almost impossible to get it either in or out when once put together.

[Length, 17 ft. 6 in.   Width, 2 ft. 9 in.   Height, 2 ft. 10 in.

Drapers' Hall, Shrewsbury.]

FIG. 12.—A SMALL SIDE TABLE IN OAK (*c.* 1675).

The plain column type turning and the square stretchers might be of earlier date, but the drawers have dovetailing and bottom runners corresponding with much work of the Restoration period. It is important to note that the drawers fit tight under the top without a lock rail in the framing, a feature peculiar to the seventeenth century.

The top is of $\frac{5}{8}$ in. oak and has the thumb-moulded edge. It is secured to the framing with oak dowel pegs.

Width, 2 ft. 9 in. Depth, 1 ft. 10 in. Height, 2 ft. 3 in.

The property of the Author.

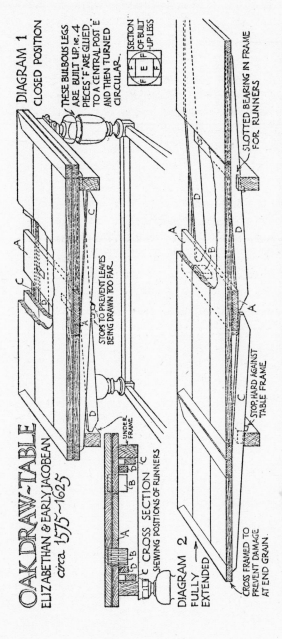

OAK DRAW-TABLE
ELIZABETHAN & EARLY JACOBEAN circa 1575-1625

DIAGRAM 1 CLOSED POSITION

THESE BULBOUS LEGS ARE BUILT UP. ie. 4 PIECES 'F' ARE GLUED TO A CENTRAL POST 'E' AND THEN TURNED CIRCULAR.

SECTION OF BUILT UP LEGS

SLOTTED BEARING IN FRAME FOR RUNNERS

STOPS TO PREVENT LEAVES BEING DRAWN TOO FAR

STOP HARD AGAINST TABLE FRAME

UNDER-FRAME

C CROSS SECTION C SHEWING POSITIONS OF RUNNERS

DIAGRAM 2 FULLY EXTENDED

CROSS FRAMED TO PREVENT DAMAGE AT END GRAIN.

THESE TABLES ARE CONSTRUCTED WITH STOUT UNDER-FRAME AND STRETCHERS UNITING THE FOUR LEGS. USUALLY, THE PLANK 'A' IS PLACED TRANSVERSELY CENTRAL AND FIXED DOWN TO THE UNDER-FRAME; THIS MEMBER HAS TWO RECTANGULAR SLOTS CUT THROUGH IT WHICH ACT AS GUIDES TO TWO HORNS 'B'. THESE HORNS—ORTUSKS,—ARE HOUSED INTO, AND PROJECT BENEATH THE UNDER SURFACE OF THE MAIN TABLE TOP, TO WHICH THEY ACT AS RIDING ANCHORS WHEN THAT MEMBER GRADUALLY RISES AND FALLS DURING THE OPERATION OF DRAWING OUT THE TWO UNDER LEAVES. WHEN THE TABLE IS CLOSED, EACH UNDER-LEAF IS IN LINE WITH THE CENTRAL PLANK 'A'. BOTH LEAVES HAVE TWO LONG ARM RUNNERS FIXED ON THEIR UNDERSIDES, MARKED C-C & D'-D, THE AFTER-ENDS OF WHICH ARE FREE, AND SLOPE AT THE CORRECT ANGLE TO PERMIT OF THE LEAVES ARRIVING AT THE LEVEL OF THE CENTRAL TABLE TOP WHEN DRAWN OUT. THE LEVERAGE ON THE EXTENDED LEAVES BEING COUNTERACTED BY THE RUNNER ENDS BEARING ON PLANK 'A'.

continued with but little alteration right through the seventeenth century and into the eighteenth, many of the later pieces showing the influence of walnut designs, such as twist-turned legs and flat-shaped stretchers, which in some were placed diagonally.

The stools and forms—the latter being of massive trestle type, as at Abbot's Hospital, Guildford, or like an elongated stool—were frequently made in sets en suite with the table, and were of such a size that when not in use they were placed under the table and rested on the stretchers.

The construction and design of turning and carving on these stools followed the character of the table to which they belonged; they also have one peculiarity of design: they are framed up with deep rails under the board seat and stretcher rails a few inches off the ground, but the legs straddle outwards, as seen from one of the narrow ends. Viewed front or back, they are parallel and vertical; also, in some cases the seat slightly inclines towards the front—*i.e.*, the side placed nearest the table (Figs. 13 and 14).

FIG. 13.—AN OAK STOOL (*c.* 1603).

The frame is deep and boldly carved with deep fluting, which is also repeated at top and bottom of the legs.

The legs are turned and fluted and the stretchers are enriched with gouge cuts. The top, though of old wood, is not original—one proof of this is the **S** *hole—neither has it the original dowel fixings.*

Top, 1 ft. 4½ in. × 10½ in.   Height, 1 ft. 9 in.

The property of the Author.

FIG. 14.—AN OAK STOOL (*c.* 1650).

The legs are very suitably turned, and illustrate the favourite habit of allowing "flats" to remain upon the circular work, as if the turner was desirous that the supports should not appear thin owing to taking too much off on the lathe.

The moulded and shaped framing is crude but very interesting, and the top, which is original, has a thumb-moulded edge. The large oak dowel pegs can be clearly seen.

Height, 1 ft. 10½ in.

Victoria and Albert Museum.

VIII.—GATE-LEG TABLES

THESE mark a complete departure from all other tables, and form a distinct chapter in English table design; also, they are probably the product of native genius, evolved through a short period of transition early in the seventeenth century.

They became extremely popular for use both in large and small rooms, and were made in very large numbers in oak and in walnut, and to a certain extent in mahogany in the eighteenth century; but throughout the three periods oak continued to be the wood chiefly employed. Another important point is that some of the simpler designs and turning employed on late seventeenth and early eighteenth century examples were reproduced in country districts by generation after generation of craftsmen until their decline in popularity at the opening of the nineteenth century.

There are about twelve different types known, some being very rare; the legs varied in number from four to twelve, and the shapes of the top, when extended, were square, oblong, octagonal, circular, and elliptical.

The type generally found has eight legs in two rows of four, with varied baluster turning (Figs. 17 and 18). The stretchers on many were left square, of the same scantling as the legs, and two top edges were relieved by a slight bead mould (Fig. 18). On other and richer examples the stretchers were turned, though not always to match the legs; for instance, the legs of a table *circa* 1690 may be turned with a vase surmounted by the spiral twist, while the stretchers will have turning in well-proportioned baluster forms adjusted to suit their lengths. Of the four legs on either side, two compose the gate, each gate being framed up with top and bottom stretchers, with one of the legs pivoted to the main framing. The gates swing out—right and left—to support hinged flaps.

All framing joints are the mortice and tenon with oak dowel pegs; but in the mahogany gate-leg tables the joints were not pegged, as glue was then used, and framing was cramped while it set. If design and size permitted, a drawer was usually fitted, and on some large tables two were provided. They were set in the under-framing, and had a special carriage and runner in the form of a horizontal slat of oak fixed longitudinally in the drawer space, and upon which the centre of the drawer bottom could slide; side bottom runners are known, but are rare.

The top was composed of three pieces, the centre section being secured with oak or walnut dowels, according to wood used, but in the case of eighteenth-century examples screws were generally used to secure it from underneath on the inside of the framing.

The flaps were hinged to the centre board on the under side with a pair of small wrought-iron hinges secured with nails until the introduction of screws in the second half of the seventeenth century.

The joints between these top sections were either square, groove and tongue, or rule joint, all of which were in use in the seventeenth century, but the last named superseded the others in the eighteenth century. The edges of the top were finished with a thumb mould in certain cases, but it was usually a " softened " square edge.

A page of diagrams is given explaining the features of these tables.

(a)

(b)

FIG. 15.—TWO SMALL GATE-LEG TABLES IN OAK.

An interesting comparison may be drawn between the turning of the legs.

(a) is of pre-Restoration date, probably about 1645, and illustrates a country joiner's interpretation of the simple knob turning, unvaried by any other mouldings. Also, the top is unusually thin, the iron hinges being secured with nails, which of necessity pass right through the wood and are neatly turned over on the upper face. A drawer existed originally. The feet of the gate legs have been repaired and left unturned. The top measures 2 ft. 1 in. × 2 ft. 6 in.; height is 2 ft. 2 in.

(b) is of post-Restoration date, about 1670, though retaining the early trestle foot. The turning is distinctly scholarly, and shows the influence of contemporary architectural details such as stair balusters. Also it is very uncommon in possessing but four legs, two of them belonging to the single gate. The top is hinged to fall vertically. Again, the top is very thin; it is an oval, 2 ft. 4 in. × 2 ft. Height, 2 ft. 2 in.

(a) The property of H. Hendry, Esq.   (b) The property of Edward Hudson, Esq.

(a)

(b)

FIG. 16.—TWO GATE-LEG TABLES IN OAK OF TRESTLE-FRAME TYPE (c. 1660).

(a) is comparable with Fig. 15 b in having a turned baluster for each main support. The gate legs and stretchers are fret cut to simulate the profile of twist turning.

(b) has fret-cut and pierced, flat, baluster-shape supports, also with shaped feet and fret-cut base board ; in this example the latter is pierced. The gates again imitate the twist outline.

(b) The property of Ernest Lawrence, Esq.

[Top, 3 ft. 9 in. × 3 ft. Height, 2 ft. 4 in.

FIG. 17.—A GATE-LEG TABLE IN OAK (*c.* 1670).

A very small example possessing well-turned legs and stretchers. The top is quite thick for the size of table, but appears thin owing to the cutting back of the edge on the underside. The drawer handle is some fifty years later. The oval top measures 2 ft. 6 in. × 2 ft. 1 in. Height, 2 ft. 1 in.

The property of Edward Hudson, Esq.

FIG. 18.—A SMALL GATE LEG TABLE IN OAK (*c.* 1675).

*This is the common arrangement with a gate on either side.
The central bearer on which the drawer runs is quite distinct. The
stretchers are square with the tiny bead mould along the top edges.
The eight legs have beautifully profiled turning very similar to stair
balustrades in contemporary houses. At the base the legs are carved
with the "Spanish" type of foot. The carved drawer face and
brackets show the lingering oak traditions.*

Height, 2 ft. 3¾ in.   Top, 3 ft. 2½ in. × 2 ft. 8 in.

Victoria and Albert Museum.

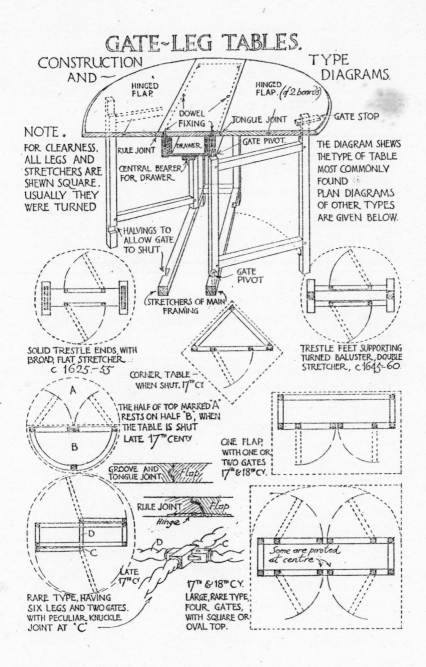

GATE~LEG TABLES.

CONSTRUCTION AND ~
TYPE DIAGRAMS.

HINGED FLAP.

HINGED FLAP. (of 2 boards)

DOWEL FIXING

TONGUE JOINT

GATE STOP

RULE JOINT

DRAWER

GATE PIVOT.

CENTRAL BEARER FOR DRAWER.

NOTE.
FOR CLEARNESS.
ALL LEGS AND
STRETCHERS ARE
SHEWN SQUARE.
USUALLY THEY
WERE TURNED

THE DIAGRAM SHEWS
THE TYPE OF TABLE
MOST COMMONLY
FOUND
PLAN DIAGRAMS
OF OTHER TYPES
ARE GIVEN BELOW.

HALVINGS TO
ALLOW GATE
TO SHUT

GATE
PIVOT

STRETCHERS OF MAIN
FRAMING

SOLID TRESTLE ENDS, WITH
BROAD, FLAT STRETCHER.
c 1625-55

CORNER TABLE ~
WHEN SHUT. 17™ C.Y.

TRESTLE FEET SUPPORTING
TURNED BALUSTER, DOUBLE
STRETCHER., c 1645-60.

A

B

THE HALF OF TOP MARKED "A"
RESTS ON HALF "B", WHEN
THE TABLE IS SHUT
LATE. 17™ CENT.Y

ONE FLAP,
WITH ONE OR
TWO GATES.
17™ & 18™ C.Y.

GROOVE AND
TONGUE JOINT

Flap

RULE JOINT

Flap

Hinge

D

C

D

C

LATE
17™ C.Y.

RARE TYPE, HAVING
SIX LEGS AND TWO GATES.
WITH PECULIAR KNUCKLE
JOINT AT "C"

17™ & 18™ C.Y.
LARGE, RARE TYPE.
FOUR GATES,
WITH SQUARE OR
OVAL TOP.

Some are pivoted
at centre

29

IX.—CHAIRS

It was not until the sixteenth century had passed that chairs were made in large quantities; chairs are mentioned in inventories of sixteenth-century yeomen's houses, but it is probable that prior to about 1600 they were scarce except in the great houses, where, chiefly as armchairs, their use was restricted to the master and mistress when sitting to table, and possibly a few would be placed in the solar and principal bedrooms; for the rest of the company stools and forms sufficed.

Nearly all these chairs had shaped arms, and, according to Mr. Percy Macquoid, between 1570 and 1620 all chairs had panelled backs with the exception of a few of X formation, following an old Gothic type.

Many examples were dated, and show this panelled type to have been made throughout the seventeenth century; the later chairs were all country made, and well overlapped the fashions in walnut.

In some early specimens the legs were left square, the space beneath the seat being enclosed with panelling, the front panel or the seat being hinged, so forming a cupboard; but in the succeeding type the front legs were baluster turned, or with the ball, reel, and knob forms, and continued above the seat with more turning as a support for the arms, the latter being of rectangular section, shaped, with rounded ends, and set at an angle which gradually became steeper (Figs. 19 and 20). Flat, rectangular rear legs continued up as back supports and raked backwards.

The back was framed up with one or two panels, generally carved, the framing being moulded, carved, or

30

FIG. 19. — A LATE ELIZABETHAN ARMCHAIR CONSTRUCTED
IN OAK AND VERY BEAUTIFULLY INLAID (MARQUETRY CUT
IN THE SOLID).

*This specimen is an early example of the over-riding top rail
with side ear-pieces. In addition to the marquetry design, its
date is established by the general proportions, the character of the
turning and grooving on the legs, and to some extent by the arms
which are set more horizontally than in the majority of later
chairs.*

Victoria and Albert Museum.

FIG. 20.—AN OAK CHAIR DATING FROM ABOUT 1630.

The top rail has here assumed the proportions of a rather over-powering cresting with heavy ear-pieces. The carving is in low relief and entirely covers the surfaces of the back and the seat framing.

The leg turning is typical of Jacobean baluster forms prior to the Restoration.

Victoria and Albert Museum.

FIG. 21.—TWO OAK CHAIRS OF THE COMMONWEALTH PERIOD WITH PANELLED
BACKS RICHLY CARVED IN PREVAILING FASHION.

*In both cases the arrangement of stretchers is identical—the front member being
turned to correspond with the turning of the legs; that of the left-hand specimen
showing a distinct advance on the many simple knob and reel forms. It is dated
1657.*

FIG. 22.—TWO CHAIRS OF THE COMMONWEALTH PERIOD WITH UPHOLSTERED BACKS AND SEATS COVERED IN LEATHER AND STUDDED WITH BRASS-HEADED NAILS AROUND THE EDGES.

The frames are in oak, with turning of ball and reel types confined to the front legs and the front stretcher. In the armchair the back uprights are ball turned at the angle above the seat.

inlaid. Particular attention was given to the top rail, which, in the sixteenth-century chairs, was usually fixed between the uprights and tenoned into them; whilst early in the seventeenth century it was placed either to ride across the uprights as a cresting, the latter being tenoned up into it, or the cresting began to extend on either side, and ears or brackets were added to the sides of the uprights. These latter features, however, are known on late Elizabethan armchairs, but under the Stuarts became more exaggerated, with carving showing a gradual decline in character and skill of execution (Fig. 20).

Rectangular stretchers, in some cases moulded, united the legs, and the seat board was thin and quite flat, often with a slight mould on its projecting edge.

About the time of the Commonwealth single chairs—*i.e.*, those without arms—came into considerable use. The construction of the seat and leg framing was similar to the larger chairs, but there was a tendency to fix the front stretcher higher up the legs and to ornament it by turned mouldings (Figs. 21 and 22). On some chairs there were two rows of stretchers.

The back was rarely panelled after *circa* 1655, the usual cross-members being rails, straight or arched, and generally carved. The tops of the back uprights were shaped or turned (Fig. 23).

About 1650 the seat boards, instead of oversetting the rails, were in some examples framed in, so providing a shallow sinking for a flat cushion or squab (Fig. 23). At this date there was also much applying of split, turned bobbins to the faces of the back uprights (Fig. 23). Chairs were becoming lighter in construction, and as the century advanced more use was made of turning, carving being confined to enrichment of the back, which was becoming lower and with arms perfectly straight, though the tall back appears again on country chairs, *circa* 1670–1700 (Fig. 23).

During the Commonwealth the foreign upholstered chairs were copied from some imported examples, so that many were made with stuffed-over seats and backs, and covered in leather, turkey work, or needlework, secured at the edges with large brass-headed nails (Fig. 22).

Until about 1660 the turning was generally in simple baluster forms, though more scholarly in proportions and detail than the earlier designs; also the knob, ball, and reel types were still popular. But about this date the early hand-cut twist or spiral was attempted in oak, though it is considered very rare prior to the Restoration, when it was improved by the lathe-turned twist. This point will be discussed in dealing with walnut furniture. Towards the end of the Commonwealth the number of stretchers appear to have been decreasing; on many chairs there was one at each side, another placed transversely and connecting them at their centres, also one in front and possibly one at the back, placed half-way up the legs. Frequently all were turned, plain squares being left on legs and stretchers, where they were mortised and tenoned one to another; on these squares all arrises and corners were rounded off. This type of chair was very popular, and continued throughout Charles II.'s reign, many being made in walnut. It is generally safer to date those having twist turning as post-Restoration. Oak chairs subsequently followed contemporary walnut fashions, and were continued in use by the more conservative or poorer inhabitants.

FIG. 23.—TWO OAK CHAIRS OF COUNTRY ORIGIN.

That on the left is a type peculiar to Derbyshire and Yorkshire where they were made (c. 1650–75), the carving and shaping of the back rails showing Continental influence.

The chair on the right has much about it that is similar in style to the fashionable walnut caned chairs of about 1675–80, particularly the type of turning, the carved rose, and the scrolling of lower rail of the back.

Victoria and Albert Museum.

FIG. 24.—A TYPICAL "OAK" BEDSTEAD, DATED 1593.

In this instance constructed in walnut and inlaid with marquetry. This illustration clearly shows the low bed frame secured at head to the head framing and standing free of the columns at the foot.

The continuous groove in the rails contains a series of holes through which the ropes passed in securing the canvas mattress.

Observe the quaint attempt at classic detail in the carved "Ionic" caps to the columns also the Elizabethan rendering of a classic cornice.

Height, 7 ft 6 in.   Length, 7 ft. 11 in.   Width, 5 ft. 8 in.

Victoria and Albert Museum.

X.—BEDS AND CRADLES

OF beds, none earlier than the second half of the sixteenth century have survived intact, and particularly of this period it can rightly be said there were beds and beds; the one a marvellously ornate structure, with panelled and carved head framing supporting the returns of a richly carved and moulded cornice, and a like tester frame, the front corners of the tester being supported by huge oak columns swelling out into one or more bulbous forms, often topped with crude Ionic caps, the shafts fluted, gadrooned, or enriched with arabesques and strap work. These columns were carried on pedestals with moulded caps and bases, panelled on all sides and often carved also (Fig. 24).

The bed frame itself was very low, and was attached to the head framing only; at the foot it stood free on its own stumpy legs. The side rails were holed and grooved for the cord lacing by which the stout canvas or rush-matting mattress was held taut, and, incidentally, this held the tenons of the side rails securely in their mortices in the corner posts. Richly embroidered hangings and curtains completed an effect of true magnificence.

The other, a very simple but pleasing affair, though devoid of tester and columns at foot, being, as a matter of fact, very much like some wooden beds of to-day, except that head and foot were connected by oak side beams holed as already described.

The head, about 4 feet high, was simply panelled and sometimes carved. The foot was very low, in some cases embellished with a row of short turned balusters between rails, the corner posts being stout and usually turned.

C   33

OAK FURNITURE

These were the English beds, and it was not until the Restoration that the few Italian importations of the first half of the century began to influence native work, when there sprang up a fashion to make less of the carved oak and more of the upholstery; consequently, the great columns gave place to more slender posts entirely obscured with rich curtains.

There are some very interesting examples of seventeenth-century oak cradles in the Victoria and Albert Museum, South Kensington.

They take the form of a low rectangular box, generally rising at one end in a shaped hood. There are posts at the corners, finished at top with a turned finial, and the four sides are panelled similarly to the chests. Under the ends cross-bearers are fixed, shaped as rockers. On those more carefully finished an inscription and date are often found (Fig. 25).

With cottagers they continued in use throughout the eighteenth century.

FIG. 25.—AN OAK CRADLE DATED 1641.

Constructed with panelled framing on the same principle as contemporary chests. The mouldings are worked "on the solid" being mitred at the top corners, and at the bottom of the stiles are cut back to fit the continuous splay on the bottom rail.

The dowel pegs can be clearly seen.

Length, 3 ft. 1 in.   Width, 1 ft. 4 in.

Victoria and Albert Museum.

FIG. 26.—OAK DRESSER.

An oak dresser dating from the second half of the seventeenth century and representing the last phase of design in the age of oak. Its late date is determined by the building up of the drawer faces with a mitred border moulding and richer panel moulds, which are mitred in a pleasing variety of shapes and all planted on, with thin flat filling in pieces, the style of work frequently and indifferently copied in so-called "Jacobean" reproductions. The carving of the split and applied turning and the acanthus brackets are sure evidence of date, as also is the large cavetto moulding fixed under the projecting edge of the top. The turning of the front legs and the thin stretchers are also post-Restoration work. The very thin top boards reflect an earlier tradition ; they are fixed with oak pegs as are the joints of the framing.

Length, 5 ft. 5 in.   Depth, 1 ft. 6 in.   Height, 2 ft. 7½ in.

FIG. 27.—A FINELY DESIGNED DRESSER IN FIGURED OAK (*c.* 1700).

The architectural influence is apparent even in this, a country made piece. Note the attached columns, the very well moulded cornice and plinth, and the breaking forward of these moulds above and below the columns. The arched doors also are good and have the coffered panel with splayed borders. The sides have panels of similar section. The drawers show an early use of the cock-bead edging and together with the doors have a cross-banded border of walnut which curves inward at the corners. The handles are of later date and obviously unsuitable on the cupboard doors. The oak is of light colour and beautifully figured.

[Width, 5 ft. 10 in.   Depth, 1 ft. 9 in.   Height, 2 ft. 11 in.

Victoria and Albert Museum.]

FIG. 28.—AN OAK DRESSER (*c.* 1780).

The lower part is fitted with three drawers, edged with the lip mould and cross-banded mahogany borders. The front legs are cabriole of quaint country workmanship. The upper part is fitted with shelves and two side cupboards, the latter being treated as the drawer fronts, and in addition inlaid with a central oval patera. The dentil cornice is typical of contemporary cabinet work, and the frieze has a fret-cut edge which rhymes with the framing of the lower part.

Width, 6 ft. 4 in. Lower part, 2 ft. 9 in. high x 1 ft. 5 in. deep.
Upper part, 4 ft. 2 in. high x 6 in. deep.

The property of H. Avray Tipping, Esq.

XI.—DRESSERS

THESE appear to have developed into the well-known form in the seventeenth century from the mediæval types, and were made for use in the smaller houses of squires, farmers, and tradesmen.

They were similar to the long side tables, with the addition of drawers and cupboards beneath the top. They exhibit the characteristics in mouldings and enrichment of contemporary work on other furniture, and many examples exist dating from the second half of the seventeenth century (Fig. 26).

During the walnut period, when carving was little employed, the oak dressers were in some cases enriched with cross-banded borders in walnut around drawer edges, etc. (Fig. 27).

During the eighteenth century a few were made in mahogany, but oak was always the prevailing wood.

Current fashions of fine furniture were constantly naïvely copied on the country dresser, the cabriole leg enjoying a great vogue, and later fret cutting and inlay.

The top part, with shelves and small cupboards, was an eighteenth-century feature, and when in original state they never have back boards, being fixed to the plaster or panelling on the wall, or standing upon the lower part (Fig. 28).

4   6   5

FIG. 29.—WROUGHT-IRON MOUNTS OF TUDOR AND EARLY
JACOBEAN FURNITURE.

*No. 1 came from an ancient building in Guildford and is of Gothic
form.*

*Nos. 2 and 3 are finely shaped cock's-head hinges used on doors in
panelling and on cupboards, etc. (c. 1560–1640). From the Isle of
Wight.*

*Nos. 4 and 5 are simple hinges used on cupboard doors (c. 1575–
1700). From an old house in Duke Street, St. James, W.*

No. 6 is an interesting lock plate early seventeenth century.

The property of Stanley J. May, Esq.

Part II

THE PERIOD OF WALNUT FURNITURE
(*Circa* 1660–1720)

I.—HISTORICAL NOTE

THE comparatively short period during which the mass of English furniture was made or faced with walnut is remarkable in many ways. As to the use of the wood, it may be regarded somewhat as a revival of an undoubted fashion that had existed among wealthy Elizabethans and Jacobeans before the Civil War, with whom it had been used for many of their best pieces, as a material above the level of oak—then considered the commonest and cheapest of woods.

With the Restoration it became doubly fashionable. The exiled prince and noblemen, during their sojourn on the Continent, had found walnut predominant, and of such many pieces were brought back by them. Consequently, although oak was still the staple material up and down the country, the Court ordained that walnut should be the vogue, worked in the Dutch and French styles.

British craftsmen had already become more or less accustomed to the intrusion of foreign design, even to the extent of having to work with other men who could not speak a word of their native tongue. This had taken place in the building of many of the great mansions during the last hundred years of the age of oak. Consequently, the joiners and cabinet-makers of Charles II.'s reign had, by their apprenticeship and observation, assimilated not a little of the more advanced continental ideas, though there is no lack of evidence of their struggle against the abandonment of the beloved traditions of their forbears.

The design and technique of the new styles immediately succeeding the Restoration were no small change from the executant's point of view, and, with few exceptions, about twenty years elapsed before he became proficient in such intricate work as cross-grain mouldings and the laying of veneers with its adornment of marquetry. He realized that glue must now be used in all cabinet work, that walnut wood, which he had hitherto employed as if it were oak, was to be worked very differently; many new tools were also necessary.

The art of cutting and laying veneers with and without marquetry was a specialized job in which he must have many lessons from his alien comrades before he set out to do likewise; and, lastly, he would have but little of Dutch construction, preferring his own methods, which in some respects were superior to those in use in the Low Countries.

It was just this matter of breaking away, and in applying their own insular feeling for design, that led the English cabinet-makers to those superb creations during the reigns of William and Anne in which eccentric foreign detail is conspicuous by its absence. In fact, it is not too much to say that, in the later cabinet work of the walnut period, pieces were designed with such consummate skill that they may rank with the wonderful productions of the Chippendale school.

To consider the early work in the walnut style, it is necessary to retread the last lap of the oak period. The date 1660—the first year of Charles II.'s *de facto* reign—marks no sudden and violent change in the nation's furnishing; for a century or more walnut wood had been used in " oak " shapes, and during the last ten years of Cromwell's rule, when he was residing at Hampton Court and undoubtedly taking some interest in the many beautiful things he retained for his own apartments, the use of walnut was rapidly growing in favour, and the first attempts at twist turning were appearing on chairs, etc.

In the early years of the Restoration it is safe to conclude that walnut was confined in native work to solid pieces, as chairs, stools, day-beds, etc., on which the legs and rails would be twist turned, together with carving, within rectangular outlines, of acanthus leafage, roses, cupids, etc., on front stretchers and back rails, coupled with the use of a newly imported material—cane—for seat and back panels.

Whatever there were of cabinets, chests of drawers, etc., in use during this reign, ornamented with veneers and marquetry, they were, with few exceptions, Dutch importations. The first veneered English pieces containing drawers invariably had the "common" dovetail at the front corners, but this was soon rejected for the "lap" dovetail as shown in the diagram.

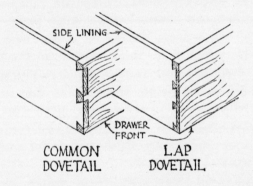

COMMON DOVETAIL   LAP DOVETAIL

The remarkable rise in the standard of comfort—almost to the level of our own—which came about at the end of the seventeenth century was responsible for the demand for a number of articles of furniture hitherto practically unknown in the country, such as chests of drawers on stands, writing and other cabinets, book and china cabinets with glazed doors, mirrors in veneered frames, long-case clocks, bureaux, and from about 1700 washstands and powdering stands, tallboys, and toilet mirrors in addition.

Naturally, the demand for these things was readily taken advantage of by the cabinet-maker, eager to exercise his skill; and that his success was so marked was largely due to his surroundings. Charles was quick to show his enthusiasm for magnificence, and the desire to have the finest and most artistic in everything necessary to his sumptuous life. He allowed—nay, encouraged—equal prodigality of expenditure amongst the women of his Court, who built and rebuilt houses for themselves, and furnished them with a stateliness and grandeur that, according to Evelyn, far outshone the quieter scheme of the Queen's apartments.

To these women, as Mr. Macquoid reminds us,* must be attributed a great influence upon decoration and furniture during the reign of Charles II.

However, this patronage of the arts by a dissolute Court was not a good thing (except in so far as it stimulated the demand for a great amount of work), and it would undoubtedly have led to absurd and debased ideas, but for the refining influence of contemporary English architecture—then at the zenith of the Renaissance.

The Great Fire of London, 1666, in which was lost scores of famous buildings—including the Gothic cathedral of St. Paul and many halls of the ancient City companies, not to mention a vast quantity of fine old oak furniture—provided an unique opportunity for the great architect, Sir Christopher Wren, to whom the rebuilding of the cathedral and over fifty of the City parish churches was entrusted.

It would be idle to suppose that the great work of rebuilding the City, which extended well into the eighteenth century, was not of the greatest importance to the joiners and cabinet-makers. London, as the centre of building activity and fashionable cabinet-making, would attract large numbers, and many would be directly engaged upon the new buildings. All would have the full maturity of the Renaissance impressed upon them, and become conversant with its rules governing mass and proportions, and such precise details as cornice, architrave, and plinth moulds.

* P. Macquoid, " The Age of Walnut."

These matters, duly assimilated, would provide a most excellent basis for setting out the lines of their cabinets, chests, and bookcases, etc. It is, therefore, in the important cabinet work of this and the ensuing period that we find the motifs of the architect adopted and incorporated.

These days also saw the rise to fame of Grinling Gibbons. This man of humble origin—a chance discovery by Evelyn—was destined to create and lead an English school of carving, the work of which, though impossible of adoption on the contemporary veneered furniture, was actually the foundation of the superb carving on mahogany furniture of the eighteenth century.

In comparing the work of joiners and cabinet-makers in the oak period, we observed that both their materials and their methods were in the main identical—*i.e.*, both used oak and both constructed on the panel principle. With the development of the walnut style this no longer obtained.

The joiner continued to use oak and frame his panels,* whereas the cabinet-maker of the period under review, in providing for broad veneered surfaces, did not panel except in cases of structural necessity, such as the backs of carcases and the large doors of bookcases, etc., and very often the latter had a mirror plate instead of the wooden panel. Moreover, the use of oak was now much restricted. As often as not yellow deal† was used in carcase work, but

* The wall panelling or wainscot was now fitted to much loftier rooms, and consisted of squat panels between a skirting and a dado rail, both boldly moulded; above this was a single row of very tall panels reaching to a cornice of classic profile practically at ceiling height. The panels had splayed borders, and frequently were surrounded by a projecting moulding of " bolection " type. See rooms at Victoria and Albert Museum, Kensington and Hampton Court Palaces, etc.

† This old yellow deal is probably the Norway Spruce or the Silver Fir, both extensively planted in Britain at the end of the sixteenth century. The wood of both is white as compared with the red deal or pine, and turns with age to a light shade of brown.

43

for parts taking friction wear, as drawer linings, etc., oak was always used in best work. A few large bookcases, etc., were made in oak and finished without veneer, but they appear more the work of architectural joiners than cabinet-makers. On the flat surfaces of built-up deal, etc., panel effects were obtained by the disposition of the pieces of veneer with various types of border inlay and banding.

With this radical change in construction, the use of screws was also introduced from the Continent, as nails were no longer permissible in fixing hinges, etc. Primitive screw-cutting devices had been known for many years, but in England the use of screws for woodwork—*i.e.*, for securing metal fittings to the wood—was practically unknown before the Restoration. In the second half of the seventeenth century nearly all screws were cut, or at least finished, by hand filing, and, of course, were unpointed.

The accession of James II. somewhat stemmed the tide of ruinous extravagance, though the Dutch and French feeling still dominated design. During his reign walnut furniture became fully established, and in the great houses oak was no longer tolerated, except in the kitchens, etc.

In 1685 the revocation of the Edict of Nantes caused thousands of French Protestants to seek refuge in this country, an event which operated to our advantage in several ways, for these people were a skilled and very industrious lot, who lost no time in settling down and plying their trades.

The silk-weaving industry quickly rose to a very flourishing condition, and home-made damasks and velvets more than met the demand for the upholstered chairs which by then were very fashionable amongst the wealthy. The middle classes—if such they could be termed— seldom could afford silk, but instead worked cross-stitch, petit-point, and other needlework as coverings for their chairs.

The beautiful tapestry manufactured at Mortlake,

Surrey, must be mentioned. This concern started in 1620, when James I. induced Flemish weavers to settle there under the grant of a large subsidy. It almost suffered extinction during the Civil Wars, but revived after the Restoration, and many chairs, settees, etc., were covered in this tapestry throughout the walnut period.

The Huguenot refugees naturally accentuated the French influence that had been more or less thrust upon Charles; consequently we observe, especially in chairs, many details that are French in character, and no doubt executed by Frenchmen in certain cases.

Contemporary with the use of walnut wood there was a rage for lacquered furniture. At first this was confined to work of Chinese origin imported by the great East Indian trading companies during Charles II.'s reign; but its popularity soon led to entirely English productions, like in the general appearance of the lacquered surfaces, but produced by a much easier and very inferior method.

The English lacquer enjoyed a great vogue until the end of George I.'s reign, when it appears to have somewhat declined in favour for about twenty-five years. It was revived, however, to play a part in the so-called Chinese Chippendale.

Gesso, as a finish for certain types of furniture, became popular to a degree during the last few years of William's reign, and continued until *circa* 1735. The process, which is described in the note on gesso, was used for articles to be finished in gilt.

The revolution which finally disposed of the male line of Stuart and set William of Orange on the throne was still another remarkable event in the history of walnut furniture. It meant, firstly, that the best of the arts of the Low Countries would be made prominent, fostered by the new king, and promulgated by the numerous artists and craftsmen whom he brought over in his service.

Greatest of these, from our point of view, was Daniel

Marot, of a French family of architects, who had fled the terror to Holland, and was then induced to enter the service of William and work over here. Besides houses, he designed many suites of furniture, and is best known by his upholstered chairs and couches, which have a mixed feeling for French and Dutch styles and stand almost apart from other native work. His influence, however, was not lost, and he furthered it by producing a book of designs published in Queen Anne's reign.

The Dutch influence is the most remarkable of all, and quite the most confusing to the student. This is largely due to the history of Holland for a century immediately preceding the English Restoration. The long wars of the sixteenth century—in which Dutch, Spanish, and French were embroiled until Spain acknowledged the Dutch independence in 1609—had the effect of strongly tinging Dutch craftsmanship with Spanish and French feeling, with the result that there were a whole host of varying details, as if different fashions were running concurrently. It is this complication of contemporary work which accounts for the great variety in form and enrichment to be found in English chairs, especially from 1685 to 1700, but with the accession of Anne, types became stabilized, and there was no longer a medley of conflicting motifs.

Richly upholstered furniture continued popular with the wealthy, and, as in the two previous reigns of Charles II. and James II., the exposed parts of the frames of such chairs were often entirely gilt.

Following the example of Queen Mary, who had observed the rage in France, a great quantity of needlework to be used as hangings and coverings was produced by the ladies in English homes, mostly of the petit-point and cross-stitch variety, and much of it very excellent in design, showing a fine appreciation of the strict limitations which surround decorative schemes for covers. This

46

plying of the needle, however, was soon to be curtailed owing to the change in design of chair backs in the early eighteenth century, when in the majority the seat only was upholstered.

Another fashion set by Queen Mary was the collecting of Oriental porcelain and Delft ware, of which she had a magnificent collection, chiefly at Hampton Court, where a few pieces still remain. This was displayed largely upon side tables and open shelves, such as receding tiers over the fireplaces* and upon cabinets, many of the latter being designed by Marot to receive china vases, etc.

The reign of William is chiefly noteworthy for the introduction of the cabriole leg, a form of very ancient origin in the East; it had been developed in Dutch and French work during the seventeenth century, and possibly some of the English scroll legs, *circa* 1675–1690, may be considered as transitional forms. However that may be, it appeared on chairs just prior to the opening of the eighteenth century, and had a marked effect upon construction. It remained in constant favour, and to the exclusion of almost every other type, for about fifty years.

With the death of William the royal patronage enjoyed by the arts since the Restoration received a rude check, for Anne interested herself but little in such matters, an attitude by no means shared by her wealthy subjects, who lavishly supported architects, painters, silversmiths, cabinet-makers, etc., to provide everything necessary to their new mansions.

By this time the country squires and merchants had largely cast aside the older oak fashions, and were welcoming the greater variety and elegance of veneered walnut, though in many a country town the forms of walnut furniture were copied in solid oak.

After the Restoration, people who dined fashionably,

* See special provision for this on fireplaces at Hampton Court, designed by Wren.

no longer sat down to a large table, but, instead, several small oval tables of the gate-leg type were used, and so became greatly in demand. The handy form of this table and its suitability for small parlours appealed to everyone; consequently, many of a large size were made at which the whole family could sit down to meals.

Card tables were also made in large numbers, for it was an age of gambling, and early in the eighteenth century a special type was produced with folding top and extending cabriole legs.

During the reign of Anne a good many time-honoured characteristics of design were changed; for example, the chair back, which hitherto had been contained between two parallel uprights, now became hoop-shaped, with a graceful S curve to the side uprights and a vase-shaped splat in the central space.

With this type little carving was necessary or desired, the favourite enrichments being the escallop shell on the knees of the legs and on the splat and the centre of the seat frame.

The majority of these chairs are extremely pleasing, and form ample testimony of the satisfying effect of perfect proportion and line. Another remarkable feature was the elimination of stretchers between the legs of chairs, couches, tables, and stands; they remained absent in all designs until reintroduced on the square leg, *circa* 1755.

The chief characteristics of furniture veneered in walnut are the warm golden-brown tones, appearing extremely rich under the original oil varnish and subsequent waxing, and the wonderful grain of the wood, on which much depends in obtaining the desired effects, by balancing the curved lines and markings about the centres of panels, drawer fronts, etc.; also by cross-banding the borders and frames and the clever trick of working the important mouldings across the grain.

The veneer was laid on oak in work of the first quality,

48

but that wood proved a difficult base for the permanent adhesion of veneer under changes of atmospheric conditions; consequently, yellow deal was substituted for carcase work in the majority of specimens.

Pieces in solid walnut are usually of a darker tone; there is not that transparency or life in the grain so well brought out in veneering, neither is there much strongly marked grain to be seen.

Before the end of Anne's reign it was evident that walnut furniture was very subject to attack by wood-worm, many of the seventeenth-century pieces being then badly eaten in legs, etc.

This is considered by some authorities to be one reason for the adoption of mahogany, which was becoming fashionable by 1720, though very costly; yet many veneered cabinets and bureaux and solid work in walnut, such as chairs, continued to be made side by side with mahogany until well into the second quarter of the eighteenth century.

Walnut wood in its unwrought state is no more liable to worm than many other woods, and Mr. Cescinsky* makes the interesting suggestion that the prevalence of worm in walnut furniture may be due to the saccharine matter in the oil varnish proving a tempting bait, the varnish being well brushed into the wood directly the article was finished, as a base for wax polishing.

There are, however, many genuine examples which still remain quite free from worm; one instance, forming the subject of an illustration facing page 69, is the gate-leg table belonging to Mr. Stanley J. May. It is hardly possible to say whether this specimen was varnished originally, but its surface to-day rather suggests it has always been wax polished (Fig. 56).

As regards the wood itself, it has a rather interesting

* Herbert Cescinsky, " English Furniture of the 18th Century," Vol. I.

history. Its cultivation in Europe was begun by the Romans as early as the first century A.D. for its wood and fruit. On the Continent it was largely cultivated during the Middle Ages, and was highly prized for cabinet work in Italy and France long before its adoption in England. It is supposed the Romans first planted it here, and apparently it was valued chiefly for its fruit, little being used for furniture during the age of oak. Recent research has disclosed some inventories of the sixteenth century which mention beds, chairs, stools, and tables in " walnot-tree."

It is certain the cultivation of the tree received a fillip during the second half of the sixteenth century, and this policy continued under James I. At the same time walnut wood was imported from the Continent; but it is most probable there was sufficient of mature home-grown timber to meet the great demand after the Restoration. However that may be, some authorities consider that a proportion of the furniture in solid walnut made during the reigns of Charles II. and James II. was cut from imported wood grown on the Continent; but whether this represented the major or the minor part must remain a debatable point.

The conversion of walnut timber followed on similar lines to that of oak;* in the best growths it is a hard and rather close-grained wood weighing about 6 pounds less per cubic foot than the average Cuban mahogany, its chief disadvantages being the frequent flaws in the growth, which make it very difficult and expensive to obtain in large planks, and also it is only near the centre of the tree, where the dark grain appears, that is of any value for furniture; towards the exterior the grain is very light and soft—the sap wood.

It was therefore rarely used in panelling, and except for legs and other short, solid members, was mostly cut into veneers, in which form a little went a long way.

* With the exception of water seasoning.

Much skill was displayed in arranging the angles of the cuts to obtain the richest effects of the greatly varying tones and lines in the grain.

Also the burrs (which are malformations due to injury, such as lopping, and other causes purely accidental) and the bottom of the bole against the roots were both utilized to provide veneers of considerable beauty.

The other type of veneer, known as oyster wood* was obtained by cutting across the grain of branches of the tree.

All old veneers were cut with the saw, and generally by the sawyers at the pit, who could cut six or seven out of every inch of wood. The modern veneer is mostly knife-cut on a special machine, and is a mere wafer.

Pollard walnut is timber cut from the trees that have been subject to regular pollarding, a treatment also applied to oak, elm, etc.

Tiger walnut is a term applied to cuts from certain growths displaying dark, wavy stripes in the grain.

* Probably laburnum was used more frequently than other woods.

51

II.—CHAIRS

OF all the early work of the Restoration in solid walnut, chairs represent a far greater output than anything else, and as they appear to have been made at an earlier date than other articles, it is appropriate to commence our study with them.

The use of walnut for furniture was growing in favour during the quieter times which marked the closing years of the Commonwealth, and the walnut chairs that can be placed to this time were generally turned in ball, knob, and reel forms on all members, while on a few the new type of twist or spiral is found in conjunction with the other types. Some of these twists are cut very hollow and appear slightly irregular, as if hand-made; others are sturdy and somewhat drawn-out.

The twist had been used on Dutch and Portuguese chairs from the beginning of the century, and on Italian work still earlier.

The wood-turning lathe had long been known and used, but in its plain form was incapable of turning shapes other than curves at right angles to the axis. According to Moxon's " Mechanick Exercises, or the Doctrine of Handy Works," 1680, in the section dealing with turnery, a special contrivance was fitted on the wooden lathe when it was desired to cut shapes or mouldings obliquely to the axis of the work. It was termed swash turning—" you set it to that slope you intend the swash on your work shall have "—*i.e.*, it was possible to regulate the frequency of the spiral. Moxon amplifies his directions by a wood-cut, showing a twist-cut leg or baluster in the lathe, but

52

the drawing is not sufficiently clear to understand the mechanism.

To turn a spiral to-day, a gear and slide rest are used. Some of the old spirals are " two-start " or double—*i.e.*, the tool has been started on its cutting in two separate places on the line or small moulding from which the spiral springs. On a few rare specimens (and including some balusters cut in oak in Wren's City churches) the double spiral appears as two separate and distinct twists; this was generally commenced by boring out the core of the wood longitudinally.* It also entails considerable hand-finishing.

To revert to the chairs. About 1660–1665 they appeared with all legs, stretchers, and back uprights twist turned; the latter terminated in knob finials. All these members were out of square section, and rectangular portions were left for the mortice and tenon joints by which they were framed together (Fig. 30).

The back uprights, which are continuations of the rear legs, sloped backwards to give added comfort, thereby forming a distinct angle where the upright rises above the seat (Fig. 31). This had obtained on the oak chairs, but was now becoming more pronounced until, *circa* 1680–1690, it was almost excessive (Fig. 36). The angle was a weak point, except in armchairs, and it is interesting to reflect upon the awkward task of turning both portions of these cranked members. If they be examined, it will be found that the direction of the grain of the wood is parallel with a straight line drawn between the top finial and the foot. In this way the danger of short grain at the bend was partly overcome.

The rails of the back, which at first were devoid of any cresting, and the seat frame, were of rectangular section, sometimes lightly moulded on the edge, and were holed

* The double spiral is to be seen on the legs of a small walnut table at the Victoria and Albert Museum, South Kensington.

to receive the cane panel, which in these earliest specimens was of large open mesh.

In the case of arms being added, they were at first quite flat, bowed on plan, and tenoned into the back uprights and to an upward extension of the front legs. The feet were usually circular, turned in vase or ball form.

In some of these chairs vertical slats in lieu of caning filled the back.

The seat frame was frequently incised with a lozenge or lattice pattern on the outer faces. Within the next two or three years carving was introduced, and quickly assumed an important part in the design. The front stretcher, fixed half-way up the legs, was now a flat member, 4 or 5 inches wide, on which a rather crude type of acanthus leaf and flat-petalled rose or crown were carved; this same motif appears on the top and bottom rails of the back, and also in many cases on the inner uprights to which the caning was laced at the sides (Fig. 31).

By 1670 this type of enrichment had greatly improved, the carving was varied with cherubs supporting a crown or basket of fruit and flowers, and was in fairly full relief with the background pierced (Fig. 33).

The rectangular surfaces at the joints were also carved in slight relief, and in some chairs the front legs were shaped and carved in tall scroll form (Fig. 32) instead of twist turning, which was still popular for the rest of the framing, though it must be mentioned that almost immediately after the appearance of the scrolled front legs simple baluster turning reappeared on many chairs for back uprights and side and rear stretchers (Fig. 32).

About 1670, possibly earlier, the arms were of rounded section (of the same section, in fact, as the scrolled legs); they were no longer bowed, but shaped to a hollow downward curve, and were finished with a large scroll over the front supports with leafage carved in slight relief (Fig. 31). As time advanced these scrolled ends tended to curve

FIG. 30.—WALNUT ARMCHAIR UPHOLSTERED IN FRENCH
NEEDLEWORK (c. 1660).

The low, padded back on rectangular uprights and the
simple twist turning are characteristic of English chairs in
oak and walnut in late Commonwealth and early Charles II.
work, but exactly similar chairs had been made for many
years by the Dutch. Numbers were exported from Antwerp
to this country.

In slightly earlier examples the rear legs are not turned
but remain rectangular. In this example they probably
make a joint with the back supports.

FIG. 31.—AN ARMCHAIR IN WALNUT (*c.* 1665).

The legs, stretchers, and back uprights turned with a fine type of twist or spiral; the front stretcher and also the boards framing the back panel are carved in low relief with leaf scrolls and flowers. The seat and back are caned.

Victoria and Albert Museum.

outward, so becoming more extravagant of material; their supports above the seat frame were often scroll-cut also (Fig. 32). The caning was now of finer mesh, but became still closer in the last decade of the century.

The outlines of the carving on front stretchers and back cresting were no longer restrained within parallel limits, for with the addition of S scrolls and other detail, often foliated, they rose in height at the centre, were extremely rich in effect, and admirably executed. It must be remembered that the back cresting was still between and framed into the sides of the uprights.

In some chairs possessing these features the back is filled with about three splats of carved and opposed S scrolls arranged in groups and tiers.

The seat frame was still composed of four separate members mortised into the sides of the legs, and a running leaf design was frequently carved on the exposed surfaces.

Much of the work in fine chairs of Charles II. period is decidedly French in character; in the fanciful shaping and carving of legs, front stretchers, and crestings, etc., we see the taste of such notorieties as the Duchess of Portsmouth, who was, in fact, a French woman.

Before the accession of James II. twist turning had practically died out on fashionable chairs, being superseded by well-designed baluster forms on the back uprights.

The space devoted to caning in the back was also becoming narrow, and the preference for scrolled carved forms (or simple turning) dominated the legs, many being not far removed from the cabriole shape.

The open-back chairs of James II. were taller and narrower than the Charles types. Commencing *circa* 1675 many chairs had stuffed backs, obscuring the framework, the seats also being stuffed over (Fig. 32). The covering materials were needlework, damask, or velvet, trimmed with remarkably rich fringes.

The scrolled legs were also designed for single chairs, without any square portion at the top into which the seat members could be tenoned; the seat was, accordingly, framed up separately, then let *into* the back uprights and *on to* the front legs, having a hole bored at each front corner into which the turned and tapered top of the leg could fit like a dowel, and a peg was often driven in the side of the seat frame for greater security; it was, however, a defective method compared with tenoning into mortices in the legs (Fig. 34).

On these seat frames, which are broad and thin, a round mould will generally be found on the outer faces.

The scrolled leg and carved stretcher did not completely oust turning on these front members, for *circa* 1690 chairs appeared with a swell-turned leg (Fig. 36), and a double-swell or a carved stretcher; legs also were given a sudden broadening like an inverted cup (Fig. 37), and the foot was spread like the bun feet of cabinets. In some cases there was the carved " Spanish " foot (Fig. 34).

Besides the swell-turned stretcher, other favourites were various types of moulded arch forms, sometimes with foliage in full relief (Figs. 36 and 37).

The French influence, due, no doubt, to the large numbers of Huguenots here in exile, is apparent on many fine chairs made during the short reign of James II., which revive exuberant carving. The front legs are scrolled or turned and carved, the back uprights are turned, and the back is composed of one large open carved panel with an ornate cresting fixed between or upon the uprights, which is repeated as the front stretcher. The seat was deep framed, in direct contrast to the English flat frames, and was stuffed over in damask, velvet, or cross-stitch.

Other important changes *circa* 1690 in the more English types concern the back; the cresting, in cases only slightly carved, was now riding over the uprights (the evolution of the cresting on oak chairs is thus re-

FIG. 32.—AN UPHOLSTERED CHAIR (*c.* 1680) ILLUSTRATING
THE FRENCH INFLUENCE ON LATE CHARLES II CHAIRS.

Turning is relegated to the side and cross stretchers and the rear legs. The front legs and arm supports, also the front stretcher, being carved in large **S** *scrolls with spiral ends. The carved arms are of similar section to the legs and do not turn outward at their scrolled ends.*

FIG. 33.—A FINE EXAMPLE OF A WINGED ARMCHAIR UPHOLSTERED
IN DAMASK (*c.* 1680).

*The scroll legs with narrow turned tops indicate the closing years of
Charles II.'s reign. The legs are also carved with boys' heads, and this
motif is carried further on the richly scrolling stretcher where two boys
sit astride in the position of supporters.*

*Behind this ornate front, the side and transverse stretchers are turned
with simple mouldings and the rear legs are square-ended.*

The whole of the underframing is gilt.

Height, 4 ft.   Width, 2 ft. 6 in

FIG. 34.—A WALNUT CHAIR WITH CANED BACK
AND RUSH SEAT (*c.* 1690).

*One of the more English of William and Mary types, yet not without
distinct Continental influence. There is the style of Spanish work in the
double curved ends of the caned panel, also in the lines of the cresting
and front stretcher and in the carved feet of the front legs, which are
incomplete owing to the lowest parts of the curves (formed on attached
pieces) having become detached and lost. The caning is of finer mesh
than earlier examples, but became still finer between 1690 and 1700.*

FIG. 35.—A CHAIR WITH UPHOLSTERED BACK AND
SEAT (*c.* 1695).

*This type was very popular for a few years; it shows the
moulded* **X** *stretchers, here further elaborated by arched curves.
The centre finial is also present.*

*Turnery is all but absent, mouldings on the legs being mostly
carved on square and octagonal sections.*

The covering is needlework in cross-stitch.

Compare with settee, Fig. 46.

peated later in walnut), and often partook of the moulded form of the arched stretcher; also the cane panel—very tall and narrow—has a moulded or shaped uncarved frame, with top and bottom often rounded or ogee shape (Fig. 34).

These types carried on until the end of the seventeenth century, but in fashionable circles the designs of Daniel Marot completely revolutionized the style from about 1695. In these the seat was usually upholstered, and also the back, except that many well-known examples have the space between the uprights filled with rich pierced carving composed of foliage, opposed S scrolls, etc., and capped by an ornate cresting, which is repeated in the front stretcher; the latter in some cases was not attached to the front legs, but set back a few inches and tenoned to the side stretchers at the lower level (Fig. 37).

There is much variation in the legs of Marot chairs, particularly the front pair, where turning is less in evidence than square moulded and geometrically shaped forms; also the broad inverted cup (either circular or octagonal) tapered to a small section over the rectangular block at the stretcher level, and again fattened to an octagonal or a bun foot (Fig. 35). The faces of the square cutting were often slightly sunk in panels. The frames were frequently gilt.

During the last ten or fifteen years of the seventeenth century many chairs exhibit stretchers which break clean away from the sensible rectangular construction by being arranged diagonally and serpentine in form; they are framed into the block immediately above the foot. These cross-brace stretchers are of a delicate moulded section, and are usually lap-halved where they cross or tenon into a central block, the former joint being secured with a peg which is utilized as a fixing for a turned finial (Fig. 35). They are graceful but useless as constructional ties.

This type of leg bracing is only to be found on fine

chairs, of which the majority are stuffed, though they are known in the Marot style with open back. Many were gilded, and good examples may be seen at Hampton Court.

It should be mentioned that many country-made Stuart high-back chairs had rush seats (Fig. 34), as cane was not obtainable everywhere, nor would it stand hard wear like the rush. The backs of such were generally filled with a simple arrangement of narrow slats. Simple turning characterized the legs, but the arched cresting and stretcher were often essayed.

Besides walnut, country chairs were made of oak, or beech, generally painted black.

A few years prior to the close of the seventeenth century the true type of cabriole leg was introduced from Holland, and, being a new fashion, was only adopted by the few who could keep in touch with the latest ideas and models. It is therefore contemporaneous, until the opening of the eighteenth century, with the narrow, high-backed, and caned chairs still in general use about the country, and the fine upholstered chairs with shaped legs and flat serpentine stretchers. But with the coming of this new leg important alterations are to be seen about the lines of the chairs: there was no turning; the flattish back uprights, while at first remaining vertical as seen from the front, were curved backwards in serpentine form—*i.e.*, they were convex just above the seat, and then became concave towards the top rail better to suit the back of the sitter; a carved and arched cresting rode over these uprights, though becoming more formal; and a wide-shaped splat, at first carved and pierced, filled the central space, being framed to bottom rail and cresting.

At first the front legs only were cabriole, and often without the addition of shoulder-pieces. There were three shaped stretchers, one on each side from front to back, and a cross-member joining them about midway, which was often carved also, the rear legs being square

FIG. 36.—A WALNUT CHAIR (c. 1695).

A walnut chair of about 1695, illustrating the very high narrow back at a severe inclination, which the arms greatly help to strengthen. The latter are characteristic of the last decade by reason of the pronounced outward twist of the scrolling ends.

As is usual the carved arched stretcher is repeated on the back cresting. The back has an inner pair of turned uprights and four moulded vertical slats. The swell-turned front legs and cupped feet are typical.

FIG. 37.—A VERY RICH WALNUT CHAIR (*c.* 1695)
IN THE MANNER OF DANIEL MAROT, THE FRENCH
ARCHITECT TO KING WILLIAM.

*The intermixed Dutch and French character of the finely
carved back filling and cresting, and also the low-recessed front
stretcher demonstrate the very un-English phase in our furniture
which had first commenced about 1687–89, due to the great influx
of Huguenots.*

*The front legs have the inverted cup form, also very popular at
this time on other types.*

*The seats of Marot chairs were generally stuffed over, as in
this case.*

FIG. 38 —A CABRIOLE LEG CHAIR IN WALNUT (*c.* 1695–1700).

*A cabriole leg chair in walnut, having upholstered seat and two
caned panels in the back divided by a plain splat. The uprights retain
the old tradition of parallel line but are well curved to suit the back,
and are boldly moulded and mitred in the solid to carry across a low
rail. The finely shaped cresting and the recessed Carolean stretcher
are faced with the same moulding and possess clever and vigorous
carving. The cabriole legs are one of the earliest types, with pied-de-
biche feet. The rear legs repeat a Carolean fashion in being carved as
tall scroll shapes over square plinths.*

FIG. 39.—A WALNUT CHAIR (*c.* 1705).

A typical chair of the Queen Anne period, indicating the simple Dutch forms then popular ; particularly is this manifested in the peculiar curves of the splat.

The front legs are of well proportioned cabriole form, carved with the escallop and pendant hush. The legs are connected by simple turned stretchers which in dining chairs were discontinued shortly before 1710.

The property of Stanley J. May, Esq

for the most part until about 1703–1705, when they were plain turned and ended in a club foot.

The cabriole curve was very decided, and the foot was generally hoof-shaped—the pied-de-biche. The seat was deep framed, and generally stuffed over (Fig. 38).

The next step, occurring much about the same time, marks another important change: those parallel vertical lines which had hitherto enclosed the form of the back were now rarely found, and we observe a shoulder formed on the uprights a few inches above the seat; above that the uprights together provided a hoop-shaped back, which was completed by an arched and carved cresting bar; the moulded front faces of the uprights were carried across the latter without break, and also across a connecting rail a few inches above the seat; the splat, framed into the cresting bar and this lower rail, was narrower than the first model, had a more definite and geometrical outline— somewhat like a fiddle—and was carved and pierced, but not to the same extent.

The stretchers were little altered; the cabriole leg had shoulder-pieces which were carved with an outline scroll coming from low-relief foliation on the knee. The seat was again stuffed over, but some had the new arrangement of an upholstered seat on a thin drop-in frame.

We now come to the walnut chairs of Queen Anne's reign.

The cabriole leg was quickly mastered by the English chair-makers, who at no time have showed to better advantage their keen eye for balance and proportion. A form that is capable of being very ugly unless it is just right is, on the old chairs, generally rendered to perfection, and, as might be expected, the construction of these chairs leaves nothing to be desired moreover.

The shaping of a cabriole leg is one of the few operations which must still be done largely by hand. To describe the method of the old craftsmen: firstly, a suitable length

59

of walnut (or, later, mahogany) was selected for closeness of grain and freedom from all faults and shakes—for a chair leg it might be 3 inches square and, say, 18 inches long. On two adjacent sides of this piece the outline curves would be marked, probably from a thin wooden template that had served similarly for scores before; the top or knee curves would appear about 3 inches from an end of the wood to allow of the necessary block into which the mortices would be cut to receive the tenons of the seat rails.* The next operation was to clamp one end in the bench, and with a large bow saw carefully to cut the profiles marked on the wood. The result was a curved leg of rectangular section, and it should be noted that from *circa* 1700–1715 several examples were made in which the legs were left in square cabriole form; but the usual way, and the next step, was first to place the leg in a lathe and turn the pad foot (unless it was intended to carve a hoof or claw and ball), and then again to fix in the bench and with a spokeshave and rasp to reduce the arrises to a rounded section, leaving it rough on the knee if carving was intended there. The leg was now complete, except that on either side of the knee there was an abrupt finish on a vertical face; this, as some specimens show us, was so left, on others the shape was rounded off with an applied acorn knob or turned rosette (Fig. 40), but generally—particularly in the later work—a shoulder-piece was dowelled or merely glued on at each side, partaking of a continuation of the leg curve and shaped on its under side (Figs. 39 and 41). It has the effect of supporting the seat rail, but does little more than strengthen against racking.

There were many delightful variations of the cabriole, partly necessitated by its use on several types of furniture; the best known of these will be found among the diagrams on page 61 illustrating its evolution and decline.

The stretchers were fast dying out; they remained

---

* This block would be much larger on legs intended for tables.

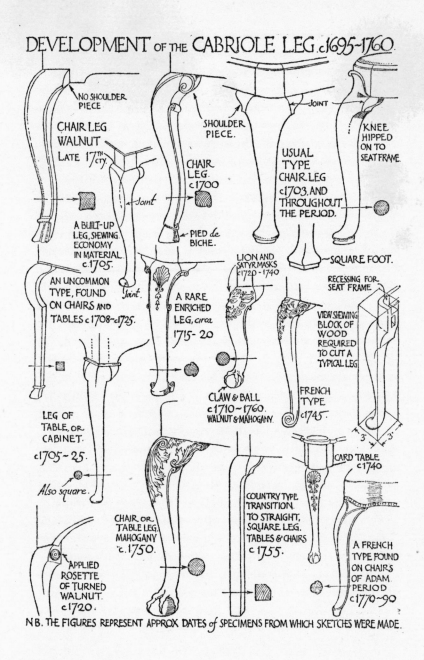

DEVELOPMENT of the CABRIOLE LEG. c.1695-1760.

NO SHOULDER PIECE

CHAIR LEG WALNUT LATE 17th C.

Joint

A BUILT-UP LEG, SHEWING ECONOMY IN MATERIAL. c.1705.

AN UNCOMMON TYPE, FOUND ON CHAIRS AND TABLES c.1708-c.1725.

Joint

LEG OF TABLE, OR CABINET. c.1705-25.

Also square.

APPLIED ROSETTE OF TURNED WALNUT. c.1720.

SHOULDER PIECE.

CHAIR LEG. c.1700

PIED de BICHE.

A RARE ENRICHED LEG, circa 1715-20.

LION AND SATYR MASKS c.1720-1740

CLAW & BALL c.1710~1760. WALNUT & MAHOGANY.

CHAIR OR TABLE LEG. MAHOGANY. c.1750.

JOINT

USUAL TYPE CHAIR LEG c.1703. AND THROUGHOUT THE PERIOD.

SQUARE FOOT.

FRENCH TYPE c.1745.

COUNTRY TYPE TRANSITION. TO STRAIGHT, SQUARE LEG. TABLES & CHAIRS c.1755.

KNEE HIPPED ON TO SEAT FRAME.

RECESSING FOR SEAT FRAME.

VIEW SHEWING BLOCK OF WOOD REQUIRED TO CUT A TYPICAL LEG.

3"   3"

CARD TABLE c.1740

A FRENCH TYPE FOUND ON CHAIRS OF ADAM PERIOD c.1770~90.

N.B. THE FIGURES REPRESENT APPROX DATES of SPECIMENS FROM WHICH SKETCHES WERE MADE.

61

longest on large upholstered armchairs, but on the dining sets they were reduced to slight plain-turned members (Fig. 39), the side stretchers being taper-fitted or tenoned into the backs of the cabriole legs, a small square block being provided in a mid position on the side stretchers into which the transverse member was framed.*

Quite a number of chairs dating from *circa* 1700 were entirely without stretchers, and after about five years they were no more employed on dining chairs until revived in a rectangular form between the square legs on mahogany chairs *circa* 1750–1755. Their rejection necessarily put all the strain into the joints with the seat frame; but seat rails were sufficiently deep and tenoned into the vertical block left at the top of the leg above the knee. The upper part of this block, together with the seat rails, were reduced in thickness to admit of a separate drop-in upholstered seat being accommodated (Figs. 39, 40, and 41). To strengthen the joints between legs and seat rails, triangular blocks were screwed into the four angles, and often utilized as a bearing for the seat. The seat framing had a small quadrant mould around the top edge, and the lower edge was sometimes shaped to balancing curves (Fig. 41).

The seat frame quickly developed characteristics: *circa* 1700 the two front corners were rounded—*i.e.*, the block forming the top of the leg followed the rounded surface made by reducing the arris on the knee—and shortly afterwards the front rail was bowed, concave, or serpentine, and the side rails were also serpentine or straight on plan, converging towards the back. The finest specimens had the seat framing, also the back uprights and the splat, veneered with finely figured walnut, being cross-banded on the former (Fig. 41).

* Usually the rear legs were plain round with square or club-turned feet; in fine specimens they were often of cabriole form. Mr. Macquoid, in " The Age of Walnut," states that it may be taken as a general rule that when back legs are club-footed and without stretchers the chair is after the date 1708.

FIG. 40.—A SIMPLE TYPE OF WALNUT CHAIR (*c.* 1708–10).

The very plain splat is inlaid with a border line of light wood, and rises from a shaped plinth.

The rear legs are also cabriole, and there are no stretchers.

Instead of fitting shoulder pieces at the sides of the knees, the flat facets are covered with round knobs glued on.

There is no quadrant mould on the top edge of the seat frame, which consequently appears thicker than usual.

FIG. 41.—A WALNUT CHAIR (*c.* 1720).

The hooped back has a dished cresting carved in low relief. The uprights and the splat are veneered on the front.

The shaped seat framing is also faced with vertical grain veneered, and has a carved shell applied on the centre of the front.

The rear legs are square with edges chamfered.

The front legs are of fine cabriole shape with claw and ball foot and shell carved on the knee.

The stuffed seat is on a drop-in frame.

Such chairs continued in use throughout the reign of George I., and in country districts until the middle of the century.

The property of Frank Partridge, Esq.

FIG. 42.—AN UPHOLSTERED ARMCHAIR (*c.* 1708).

Covered in finely designed needlework and with **C** *-scrolling arms.*

The cabriole legs are of walnut with scroll-ended beads worked on the side.

The spread of the back legs is very marked.

The feet are the pad or circular club type.

FIG. 43.—A LATE ARMCHAIR IN WALNUT (*c.* 1720).

*The shaped splat and curved uprights are veneered on front,
and the very delicate carving is a feature of the time, being cut on
applied pieces very cleverly glued down to the veneer.*

*The carving on the knees of the cabriole legs is French in
character, and is a foretaste of the fashion that was to grow in
intensity up to the middle of the eighteenth century. The shaping
of the arms and the general proportions are excellent.*

The seat has a tapestry covering.

The splat was an important and valuable part of the design, and now united the shaped top rail of the back to the seat frame; also, like the uprights, it was carefully shaped to fit the spinal curves; it rose from a shaped shoe-piece planted on the rear seat rail, and was usually profiled in beautifully balanced and proportioned curves up to the top rail, into which it was tenoned (Figs. 39, 41, and 43). Generally it was not pierced, but examples exist in which it forks at the top, to enter the head rail at two separate points.

Armchairs were made to rhyme with the various types of single chairs, and departed from the earlier traditions in that the arm supports rose from the side rails of the seat a few inches back (Fig. 43). Rarely were they a continuation of the front legs.

The arms and supports were for the most part of rounded section, serpentine in rising to their full height, then bowed and dished in the horizontal part, taken back and framed into the uprights (Fig. 43). Others (generally later examples) rode over the support, and finished in a carved scroll or volute (Fig. 48); rarely with lion or eagle head until the early mahogany period.

On a few fine examples the splat had delicate leaf carving on its edges, on others it was inlaid with marquetry, which also appeared on the front seat rail.

In examples enriched with carving upon veneered splats and rails the pieces of walnut were carefully glued down on to the veneer and then carved into leaf, scroll, or patera, the junction being so perfect as almost to avoid detection under the closest examination (Fig. 43).

Contemporary with the Queen Anne hoop back the vertical plain uprights were again revived (as found on the earliest specimens with cabriole legs), but they were now more slender and of purely round section above the seat; they were also rather tall, and the junction with the top rail is, in some cases, a right angle with the corners

63

rounded off. On these chairs the splat is often of very plain outline, sometimes delicately inlaid with marquetry (Fig. 40).

Upholstered chairs were very popular during this period, and were of two types: (1) the so-called grandfather chair with cabriole legs (Fig. 42), often with thin stretchers, the back broad and high, and fitted with forward wing-pieces and scroll over arms; (2) single chairs upholstered on back and seat, and showing no woodwork except the cabriole legs. In both types the usual coverings were needlework and velvet.

FIG. 44.—A WALNUT STOOL (c. 1720).

A beautifully designed example with cabriole legs of fine proportion, having a tiny bead carved up the sides which rolls outward in small scrolls beside the feet, and again intermediately and on the frame, which latter is cleverly shaped and retains the bead along its edge, stopped only by an escallop shell carved in the centre on the long sides. The knees of the legs are carved with the escallop shell and pendant hush. It will be observed that the fine effect is largely due to the lower member of the frame which continues part of the leg curve and is worked in cross-grain walnut.

Victoria and Albert Museum.

III.—STOOLS

To consider stools we must revert to the Restoration. There is sufficient evidence to prove that stools were still largely used during the second half of the seventeenth century. They generally had upholstered seats of rectangular or circular form, and their supports reproduced the various turned and shaped legs and stretchers of contemporary chairs; therefore, a stool may be dated according to its similarity with chairs bearing like details of design (Fig. 44).

The early specimens with twist turning were rectangular and frequently caned, as also were the longer and much lower bed steps. The "form" shapes also reappeared, being upholstered and having six or eight legs; they were mostly of the William and Mary period, and several can be seen at Hampton Court. They were known as "seats."

IV.—SETTEES—DAY-BEDS

THE settee or couch had been known for some years
prior to the Restoration; such examples had framing
resembling contemporary chairs and upholstered in leather
or turkey work.

With the introduction of caning the day-bed became
fashionable—an elongated caned stool on six or more
legs with corresponding stretchers.

At one end the two legs continue up, very much cranked
at the seat block to form a sloping support. This end
had either a fixed caned panel or one hinged by wooden
dowels between its bottom rail and the side " uprights."
The angle was thus adjustable and secured by cords or
chains at the top (Fig. 45).

The day-bed exactly followed the evolutions of the
chairs, and during William III.'s reign became entirely
upholstered. It also developed into a wider edition of
the high-backed, upholstered chair with padded arms,
etc., so forming a complete settee (Figs. 46 and 47); such
were very rare prior to 1689.

From about 1708 the walnut hoop-back chair was used
as a model for a new type of settee (Fig. 48), formed by
linking two or three normal chair backs with uprights and
with arms at the ends.

The cabriole legs also appeared at intermediate
positions under the seat rail immediately in front of the
back supports.

The back members and the seat rails of these settees
are usually found overlaid with veneer of finely figured
walnut, the top rail and the edges of the splats often

66

FIG. 45.—A WALNUT DAY-BED (c. 1670).

Designed in the Carolean style with strong French and Dutch influence, the legs being carved in long scrolls, connected with S-scroll stretchers supporting the crown and rose at the sides, and with turned stretchers at the ends similar in profile to the raking supports of the pivoted back panel. The latter has an S-scrolled frame with carved muntin and an elaborate cresting. There are two cane panels to the back rest and the seat is also caned. The damask-covered cushion and squab are original.

FIG. 46.—A WALNUT SETTEE UPHOLSTERED IN NEEDLEWORK (c. 1695).

It partakes of the three-chair-back form and retains its original covering material. The octagonal-shaped front legs and the scrolling stretchers are identical with the chair (Fig. 35).

FIG. 47.—A WALNUT SETTEE OR SOFA (c. 1715–20).

The cabriole legs have a small moulding worked on the rectangular section a few inches below the knee. The central leg is of curious shape due to the difficulty of adapting an essentially corner treatment to a flat frame. The seat frame is cut away somewhat to lighten the effect. The arms scroll over and swing down in front to short vertical scrolls, a finish in vogue from c. 1670, but going out of fashion.

FIG. 48.—A TWO-CHAIR-BACK SETTEE (c. 1715).

The seat frame is double serpentine in front with corners very much rounded, due to the shell carving on the knees of the cabriole being "swept" up on the topmost portion of the leg which receives the tenons of the deep seat framing The carved masks are glued to the rails and are very rare in this position. The front legs are of graceful outline and terminate in a square club or hoof form.

The late developments in walnut chairs are to be seen in the scroll-ended arms, and the treatment of the splat, which rises from a carved plinth, has scrolled shaping at the sides and also at the cresting, where it is formed to a hollow curve. This style of settee was made in walnut and mahogany.

The property of Percival D. Griffith, Esq.

delicately carved, the arms scroll-ended or carved with heads, the cabriole legs carved with the escallop shell and husk on the knees, and the feet with claw and ball, or turned pad shape. Stretchers are known on some specimens, and, rarely, the back is stuffed in to agree with the drop-in seat.

A lacquered finish is also known on settees of this period as well as on the normal chairs.

V.—TABLES

THE many varieties of tables were largely in solid walnut, and must next receive consideration. It will be well to return a few years to pick up the threads of design of gate-leg tables.

It was perfectly logical that the popular twist turning of the Restoration should be found on the legs and stretchers of these tables, though simple turning still persisted and oak by no means went out of use, though unfashionable.

The description of the earlier oak models applies to those of the second half of the seventeenth century, with the exception that the trestle type was almost at an end. The greater variations in design can be studied on the page devoted to diagrams.

It appears that twist turning persisted longer on the legs of these tables than on chairs, for during the reigns of James II. and William III. many fine specimens were made in which the twist rises above a vase form, and the spiral now had a more architectural feeling, being given a column-like entasis which rhymed with a gradual diminish in the proportions of the spiral (Fig. 49). The vase form was also used when the twist was not employed, and is then found in conjunction with well-proportioned contrasting curves, one member of these frequently being the inverted cup shape (Fig. 50). Many of these post-Restoration tables had their flap hinges secured with screws for the first time, though the nail was still commonly used on country-made specimens (the central portion of the top being still secured with dowel pegs).

FIG. 49.—A GATE-LEG DINING TABLE IN OAK (*c.* 1690).

The eight legs are finely turned with diminishing spirals over a vase form. The stretchers are boldly moulded spindle shapes.

A drawer is fitted on each side, running on bottom bearers.

Dimensions of top, 5 ft. 2½ in. × 4 ft. 2 in.   Height, 2 ft. 5¾ in.

The property of Ernest Lawrence, Esq.

FIG. 50.—A GATE-LEG TABLE CONSTRUCTED IN SOLID WALNUT
(*c.* 1690).

It is of the usual type with eight turned legs and two gates. The vase feet are seldom found so well preserved, also there is no worm in the whole piece. The drawer it originally possessed is missing, but the central bearer, of oak, upon which it ran can be distinctly seen. The moulded stretchers are much worn by friction with sole leather.

Top, 3 ft. 7 in. × 3 ft. 3 in.   Height, 2 ft. 5 in.

The property of Stanley J. May, Esq.

As already stated, they were now used for meals, and many were of large dimensions and with four gates; others were made as two distinct and semicircular units, which could be butted together or pulled apart to admit of the insertion of a rectangular central table, also on a gated frame. This last portion with gates shut would, when not in use, form a narrow side table, and such are sometimes found to-day separated from the end portions.

The largest and the very small tables are now distinctly rare, the latter being the most sought after.

To obviate the top boards of the very small models appearing too thick they were generally splayed back on the under side around the edge.

Some specimens of gate tables made about 1700 followed the fashion of many side and centre tables in having flat-shaped stretchers, the gate hinges being formed in the wood where the dowel pivot was not applicable (Fig. 53).

The small tables with rectangular fixed top were also receiving much attention; to a great extent their legs followed the chair-leg developments, but the flat stretchers came into use on tables perhaps a little earlier—*i.e.*, *circa* 1675–1680.

Those first made after the Restoration had twist legs and stretchers, then baluster turning became very popular, to which the flat-shaped X stretchers were soon added instead of the older method of framing them in from leg to leg.

On certain tables of very small dimensions and light construction the X stretchers were very delicate, and much like those of moulded section on contemporary chairs. But on those of more usual size—say 3 feet or more wide—the stretchers were generally designed on a different principle. Firstly, they were larger and of plain flat section (about 3 inches wide and 1 inch thick), and at their extremities broadened out into a flat square,

69

which was utilized as a seating for the leg. There were three general types:

(*a*) The serpentine curved **X**, with a finial at the cross-over.

(*b*) A **Y**-shape at each end of the stretcher connected by a central shelf of circular or oval form, intended for a metal or china bowl (Fig. 51); and

(*c*) A reversion to the older plan of four stretchers, running from leg to leg, but with the new square widening under each leg where they were lap-halved; for the distance between the legs the inner and outer edges of these stretchers were shaped in convex, concave, and ogee curves (Figs. 52 and 54).

In conformity with the table top and the main under frame these three types of stretchers were frequently veneered in cross-banded walnut; also, they were built up as a separate unit, a central hole being bored through the flat square corners or extremities, which accommodated a large dowel to unite the leg with a ball-turned foot and thereby fix the stretcher frame.

The top, of deal or oak and dowel fixed, would have its general surface veneered in one piece or quartered with cross-banded borders—sometimes with feather or herringbone inlay. The projecting edge would be thumb moulded (now termed an ovolo mould), which would be worked in cross-grain walnut (Figs. 51, 52, and 54).

The frieze of the under frame, generally excepting tables designed for a central position, was usually fitted with one or two drawers, constructed with good dovetailing in oak or deal linings, and veneered with walnut on the front to match the top (Figs. 51 and 52).

Tables, apparently designed for dressing or writing uses, were frequently constructed with a much deeper frieze, the lower edge of which was shaped in gracefu curves balancing about the centre, at which point it became narrowest; these curves were usually edged with a tiny

70

FIG. 51.—A WALNUT MARQUETRY SIDE TABLE (*c.* 1680).

The twist and moulded legs and ball feet alone are of solid walnut. The top is veneered with borders and panel of floral marquetry in various woods, and has a cross-grain edge moulded in ovolo or quadrant form. There is one drawer in the under frame fitted tight under the top and veneered with two marquetry panels in keeping with design on the top ; there is a feathered, sand-burnt border around the drawer opening.

The veneered stretcher is Y-shaped at each end, connected by an oval widening intended for a bowl. The pear-drop handles of brass are contemporary.

Top, 3 ft. × 2 ft.   Height, 2 ft. 6 in.

Victoria and Albert Museum.

FIG. 52.—A CENTRE TABLE VENEERED IN WALNUT AND DECORATED WITH MARQUETRY (c. 169c).

The top is designed with strips forming intertwined ovals, etc., in which floral designs in marquetry are placed. The many joints of the cross-grain moulded edge can be clearly seen.

The frieze has two drawers, each decorated with a marquetry panel, and the S-shaped legs and the curved stretchers are also decorated in similar manner.

FIG. 53.—AN UNCOMMON GATE-LEG TABLE IN WALNUT (*c.* 1695).

There is only one flap, which is arranged like those on the card tables.

The two gates swing on wooden hinges (not dowel pivots) and are recessed on to the frame when shut.

It was this type of table which formed the underpart of the earliest slant-top bureaux and writing desks.

The turning of the legs should be compared with the table Fig. 50.

FIG. 54.—A SMALL WALNUT DRESSING TABLE (*c.* 1700–3) HAVING
THE CUP-TURNED LEGS IN FASHION AFTER 1690.

*The top, the frieze with drawers, and the shaped flat stretchers are
veneered.*

*The top and the drawer fronts are inlaid with panels of the fine scrolling
or seaweed marquetry which did not come into vogue before* 1700.

*The half-round moulding surrounding the drawer openings is unusually
bold.*

The arched shaping of the frieze edge is typical.

projecting bead, similar to the cock bead on drawer edges chiefly of later date.

In the centre part of the frieze a shallow drawer was fitted, and on each side, two short drawers, one above the other, or one deep drawer. The edges of the drawer openings were generally surrounded by a half-round or double reed mould, following the practice of design on chests of drawers, to the chapter on which the reader is referred for information regarding this important detail (Figs. 54 and 56). Also, as mentioned in the note on small oak tables of earlier and contemporary date, the practice still obtained of fitting the upper drawers tight under the top (Figs. 51, 52, 54, and 56).

Drawer pulls and keyhole escutcheons were now of brass, the former being peardrop or fantail shape, cast hollow and on a circular or star-shaped plate, the handle being linked to a double strip of brass or iron, which was passed through a small hole in the drawer front, then parted, pressed down, and the ends turned over and driven into the wood (Fig. 72, top row).

During William's reign some very fine ornamental tables were made, having square or octagonal cut and moulded legs with elaborate moulded X stretchers (the Marot fashion). A few small tables still exist decorated in lacquer.

During the last decade of the seventeenth century the turned leg was designed with bolder baluster forms, and also the inverted cup shape, which, needing wood of greater breadth to permit of it being turned and to avoid considerable waste, was contrived by gluing on pieces to take the " cup " or by turning this portion on a separate member and then dowelling on to the much thinner part beneath (Fig. 54).

The twist legs frequently reappear, often as a spiral column over a vase shape, or an upper and lower twist, separated by a ball and reel turned centre, which in certain

71

examples can be dated as early as 1675. Such legs have the orthodox architectural base mouldings (Figs. 51 and 70).

Quite another type of leg appearing on these small tables from *circa* 1675 has to be recorded. It was of square section, but S-shaped, ending at top and base in a plain scroll outline (Fig. 52). Such legs were usually placed to face outwards at an angle somewhat less than 45°, which enabled the S curves to be appreciated from a central viewpoint. It was usual to veneer these legs in cross-banding, and they were often embellished with marquetry when the top was so treated. The stretchers were of flat section, running from leg to leg, and shaped on the inner and outer faces. Invariably the feet were ball turned. A few of this type, apparently of English construction, had a square block at the base of the leg where the stretchers were connected, but it is distinctly a Dutch form, and in such cases, if the marquetry be English-looking, it is practically impossible to pronounce a definite opinion as to place of origin.

Contemporary with the late seventeenth-century tables there was a peculiar fashion for bleaching the veneer, by which the very opposite of a full rich colour was obtained; the method employed to accomplish this is somewhat obscure.

Many small tables at this period with walnut veneered tops and stretchers had turned legs in solid yew tree.

With the opening of the eighteenth century and the adoption of the cabriole leg, which was peculiarly suitable to tables, we find the types becoming more distinct, according to their one particular use. To trace these completely would lead us to a date rightly belonging to the period of mahogany, but, keeping to the developments in Anne's reign, the most important was the card table, specially designed with a hinged half of the top, by which it would lie on the fixed half, and so form a side table when not in use. There were four cabriole legs, ornamented variously as contemporary chairs, two of which were capable of extension on folding portions of the oak under frame;

72

FIG. 55 —A WALNUT CARD TABLE (c. 1705–8) SHEWN WITH HINGED FLAP
FULLY EXTENDED FOR PLAY.

The fine cabriole legs are beautifully proportioned and carved, having lion claw and ball feet, and shell and pendant husk upon the knees, which are "swept" up to the cylindrical extension forming a support for the candle-stand corners of the top.

The type of hinge both for the flaps and the elbow-joint of the extending frame can be clearly seen. The frame and the rounded edge of top are in cross-grain walnut.

The usual covering for the top was green velvet : in this example needlework has been used.

The action of the underframe is explained in the diagram, page 180.

there were thus two hinges for each movable leg, one on the fixed frame and another at the elbow of the fold, which were specially made brass rule hinges (Fig. 55 and diagram, p. 180). The corners of the top, instead of being square, were formed as projecting segments of circles, with complete circles in walnut slightly sunk on the surface as positions for candlesticks. Also on all four sides an elliptical sinking was provided for money. The top was bordered and edged in cross-banded walnut, and the general surface usually covered in green velvet glued down and often secured at the edges with brass nails. The rounded corners of the top provided a reason for forming projecting rounded angles on the under frame, with which the knees of the legs were shaped to agree (Fig. 55).

These tables, excepting those of country origin, wherein the necessary balance on the leg curves, etc., is often sadly wanting, were generally of charming proportions and superb workmanship.

Other types of this period were fitted with drawers in various arrangements, and the later developments in mouldings, etc., around the edges again corresponded with contemporary work on chests of drawers.

The top was in some cases of solid wood—*i.e.*, without veneered surface—such probably being intended as washstands. The moulded edge of the top was either the large ovolo, as on earlier specimens, or had one of very much less width, confined almost to the top edge, and turned in at the corners.

The brass handles were often more elaborate than the simple peardrop; the back plate was pierced in patterns or roughly engraved, and with complex outlines; the handle itself was a cast loop often moulded, at first held by and swinging from brass links passing through the back plate, which altered later to brass knob-shaped sockets on the face of bolts which were threaded for a nut at the inner end (Fig. 72).

73

VI.—CHESTS OF DRAWERS

CHESTS of drawers veneered with walnut came into great favour about twenty years after the Restoration. They were considered worthy of the best efforts of our cabinet-makers, and many have survived in good condition, though rarely capable of being dated before 1680.

They may be divided into three general groups:

(1) Those about 3 feet 3 inches high with veneered top, containing, as a rule, five drawers, a projecting large ovolo mould around the top edge or a small cornice, and a projecting plinth mould (the latter often being an inversion of the cornice), a short vertical plinth, largely cut away, leaving bracket feet at the corners, whose inner edges were shaped; alternatively, beneath the plinth mould the supports consisted of large ball or bun turned feet.

A common practice was the placing of the top drawer or drawers right up under the small cornice, and the bottom drawer tight down on the plinth mould, which latter is found worn at the sides where the drawer has rubbed.

(2) The chest itself as No. 1, though in cases possessing only four drawers, including also the cornice and plinth moulds, but resting upon a low stand consisting of four, five, or six legs with stretchers. They rarely can be dated prior to 1689. The frieze of the stand frequently contained drawers, being, in fact, similar in all details to contemporary side tables (but lower) and following their evolutions (Fig. 56).

(3) The tallboy chest of drawers, dating from *circa* 1710, which can be subdivided:

74

FIG. 56.—A CHEST OF FIVE DRAWERS, MOUNTED UPON
A LOW STAND WITH SIX LEGS AND ALSO CONTAINING
A DRAWER (*c.* 1690).

*With the exception of the solid walnut legs, the whole is veneered
in walnut with floral marquetry of Dutch character on the
drawer fronts.*

*The cornice is of the usual small and simple section, and the
projecting edge of the stand frame is identical with edges of contemporary table tops—and in cross-grain walnut.*

*The drawer openings on the chest are surrounded with the plain,
half-round, cross-grain moulding.*

Height, 4 ft. 2½ in. Width, 3 ft. 5 in. Depth, 1 ft. 11½ in.

Victoria and Albert Museum.

FIG. 57.—A WALNUT DOUBLE CHEST OR TALLBOY (*c.* 1720).

The carcase is of deal, the front being veneered in fine figured walnut cleverly arranged with balancing figure.

The drawers have a cross-banded border and lip-mould edging. A writing slide is fitted above the drawers of the lower section, being framed of oak, which is also used for the drawer linings.

The fine cavetto cornice is entirely formed in cross (vertical) grain walnut on pine backing, as also are the other mouldings. The splayed corners fluted on cross-grain walnut. The bracket feet are also veneered. The sides are veneered in straight-grain walnut.

Height, 6 ft. 2 in.   Width, 3 ft. 3½ in.   Depth, 1 ft. 9 in.

The property of Ernest Lawrence, Esq.

(*a*) A lower portion as No. 1, but with its top mould, projecting or not, always receding inwards as a plinth for the upper chest (which also may have a small base mould in addition), and is less in width and depth than the under chest. The top chest frequently had three long drawers and a top row of three drawers (Fig. 57).

(*b*) As (*a*), but the lower chest contained fewer drawers, due to its being mounted on cabriole legs; in fact, in some examples the lower part must be termed a stand with drawers in a frieze of shaped outline (Fig. 58).

Common characteristics of the tallboys are the splayed corners, more particularly applying to the top chest, though often found on the lower chest or the stand. They were wide chamfers faced with thin cross-grained pieces of walnut, finishing at their lower ends on a graceful curve by which the splay was " stopped " and brought out to the right-angled corner. At the top the splay continued into the cornice, with which the mouldings—usually an ogee or cyma over a large cavetto—also complied. Vertical fluting or applied frets decorated the chamfer.

At this period many chests and cabinets, etc., were conceived almost as architectural compositions of a simple sort, their fine mass, proportions, and scholarly mouldings bringing them quite into line with the decorative woodwork of the rooms.

As to their construction. The carcase was of yellow deal in flat unpanelled surfaces* about 1 inch thick, formed of boards glued together with the grain, the sides, top, and bottom being dovetailed together. The horizontal divisions between the drawers were housed into the sides and extended the full depth of the chest. The angle bracket feet beneath the plinth mould, while appearing to support the chest, did not always do so; the brackets were usually mitred at the angles, and in the internal angle was placed a square block coming directly under the

* The backs were enclosed by panels or wide boards.

corner of the body and taking the weight; it also projected a fraction of an inch below the brackets.

Probably to reduce cost, and following a Dutch practice, the sides of chests, cabinets, and bureaux were sometimes left unveneered, but the better examples were overlaid with finely figured or straight-grain walnut, panel effects being obtained by laying a border strip of cross-banded veneer (*i.e.*, the grain across the direction of the band) and by the narrow feather or herring-bone inlay an inch or two from the edge. This latter consisted of a pair of very narrow strips of walnut veneer, both cut across the grain at 45° and so laid together that the grain met continuously on the line of junction, presenting the effect of a bird's feather or herring-bone.

The plinth was veneered with grain horizontal or vertical.

Early veneer was usually laid with a special tool known as a veneering hammer; but after *circa* 1690, when on curved surfaces, such as the splat or seat frame of a Queen Anne chair, a counterpart or mould of the surfaces, known as a caul, was accurately cut and shaped in another piece of wood, and with a sheet of thin paper interposed to prevent sticking, was heated and then clamped down upon the veneer until it had set. The caul and the hammer continued in use in eighteenth-century work.

The cornice and plinth moulds were always worked across the grain—*i.e.*, on the splayed deal backing a row of short and often wedge-shaped pieces of solid walnut were glued closely together, and with the grain vertical for the whole length of the member, with mitred angles. When set, the moulding plane was carefully run along to produce the required profile, a very rich and beautiful effect resulting when polished.

In the case of some chests on stands and some tall-boys the cornice was given a strongly architectural character in the following ways:

76

(*a*) There was a top projecting moulding or cornice proper, beneath which was a swell or pulvenated frieze, both in cross-grain walnut, and the latter usually the front of a secret drawer. Beneath this frieze was a very narrow moulded necking or architrave strip (Fig. 59).

(*b*) The cornice, largely composed of a cavetto with smaller members above and below, was arched, either centrally with a continuation of straight cornice on each side, or there was a double, and rarely a treble, arching of almost complete semicircles; the cavetto being in vertical veneer and the small mouldings on cross-grain facing strips.

Turned finials were often added at the corners and above the level of the mitred junctions of the arches.

(*c*) The cornice was formed as a pediment, pointed or curved, generally the latter, and of large cavetto section (Fig. 64).

It was formed in " broken " fashion—*i.e.*, with the centre part omitted, and in the gap a small stand or pedestal for a vase or turned finial. It must be mentioned that this type is very rare on tallboys, being a more usual finish on bureau bookcases, and was not adopted until late in Queen Anne's reign, *circa* 1710–1715.

The moulds around the drawer fronts are a very good indication of date, though always to be taken in conjunction with the other features.

They have been drawn in diagrammatic form, and appear on page 79 with dates of the periods during which they were in use. The figures are necessarily approximate, and it must be remembered in all such matters there was a good deal of overlapping.

It will be observed that No. 3 extends into the mahogany period. Nos. 1 and 2 were worked in cross-grain walnut.

There was a fourth treatment, not so extensively used, dating from about 1705 to 1725, in which a small projecting bead was fixed to the edges of the carcase framing around the drawer openings. This next changed into the bead becoming fixed on to the edges of the drawer fronts—the cock bead of the mahogany period; it is detailed among diagrams dealing with drawer construction (p. 177).

In various pieces of country origin, made in solid oak throughout, borders of cross-banded walnut were often let in on the solid drawer fronts (Fig. 27); and when type No. 3 was used the projecting lip mould was part and parcel of the oak front.

To return to the veneered pieces. The faces of the drawer fronts were veneered with vertical grain walnut or oyster wood ; the positions of escutcheon and handle plates were chosen to place the vertical joins in the veneer, the lines of the figure or grain being opposed about these points with added charm of effect; the borders were generally cross-banded and feathered, used either together or singly (Figs. 57 and 59).

Occasionally on examples of late date—*i.e.*, about 1730—a little strip inlay of geometrical pattern in holly and ebony was used, but it is unusual and frequently has been added subsequently or denotes Dutch work.

The drawers were of oak or deal, according to the quality of the piece; often the veneered front was deal, while the sides, back, and bottom were oak; the common dovetail, at first used at all four angles, presented too much end grain where the veneered border was laid on the face; consequently, *circa* 1685, lap dovetailing was substituted, which allowed an uninterrupted front for veneering. The top edges of the sides were usually rounded, the lower edges were either rebated or left square, and the boards of the bottom were nailed up into them; the latter were fixed with grain going from front to back.

In the late walnut chests—*i.e.*, from about 1715—the drawer sides were grooved to provide a housing for the bottom boards, as in mahogany specimens, this being illustrated on the page of drawer details.

The most costly chests, dating from *circa* 1680, had

78

DETAILS of VENEERED DRAWER FRONTS.

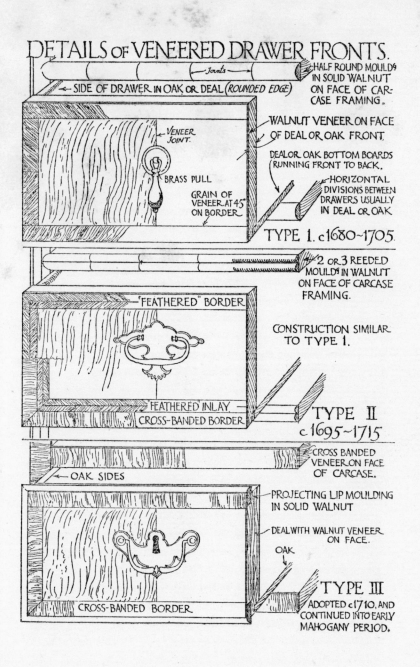

Joints

← SIDE OF DRAWER IN OAK or DEAL *(ROUNDED EDGE)*

HALF ROUND MOULDˢ IN SOLID WALNUT ON FACE OF CARCASE FRAMING.

WALNUT VENEER ON FACE OF DEAL OR OAK FRONT.

DEAL OR OAK BOTTOM BOARDS RUNNING FRONT TO BACK.

HORIZONTAL DIVISIONS BETWEEN DRAWERS USUALLY IN DEAL OR OAK

VENEER JOINT.

BRASS PULL

GRAIN OF VENEER AT 45° ON BORDER.

TYPE 1. c 1680~1705.

2 OR 3 REEDED MOULDˢ IN WALNUT ON FACE OF CARCASE FRAMING.

CONSTRUCTION SIMILAR TO TYPE 1.

"FEATHERED" BORDER

FEATHERED INLAY —
CROSS-BANDED BORDER

TYPE II c 1695~1715

CROSS BANDED VENEER ON FACE OF CARCASE.

OAK SIDES

PROJECTING LIP MOULDING IN SOLID WALNUT

DEAL WITH WALNUT VENEER ON FACE.

OAK

CROSS-BANDED BORDER

TYPE III
ADOPTED c 1710, AND CONTINUED INTO EARLY MAHOGANY PERIOD.

79

their tops (if of low type), their drawer fronts, and sometimes their sides also, inlaid with panels and borders of marquetry in veneer (Fig. 56); when this was employed, the " ground " was usually of straight-grained walnut, and sometimes in " oyster " wood. Marquetry-cutting in veneer is a skilled trade, and in best work is still done by hand, the object being to produce a design in various woods, which in the English work consisted of a gay floral pattern, until the decline—associated with marvellously clever execution—produced the close-scrolled seaweed type. A variety of tints was obtained by dyeing portions of the wood; by introducing ebony, pearl, and ivory; and also by scorching with hot sand.

As to the method employed. The design was first drawn upon paper, duplicates being made by pricking through; the pattern was then pasted on the topmost of two or more sheets of veneer which were held together with panel pins, or by glued paper interposed. The marquetry-cutter then worked along the lines of the drawing with a fine frame saw. Portions of each layer were selected, and after any requisite staining, were arranged in the spaces on the " ground," then held together by gluing a sheet of paper over the whole. After roughening its under side and the surface to be veneered, it was glued down upon the carcase. The hot caul was next applied and clamped down, or placed in the press, if suitable, for about twenty-four hours.

Another method was that in which the pattern was cut away from the " ground " layer, which was then glued in position, and out of another layer of contrasting tint (also marked or covered with the design) the leaves, birds, etc., were cut out and glued into the gaps waiting for their reception in the previously cut and fixed " ground." This needed greater skill but ensured very close joints. When thoroughly set, all paper and superfluous glue would be scraped and sanded off.

It will be realized that in each layer half would be used and half discarded; these seconds or negative portions were sometimes used in the panels of another piece of furniture, and examples are extant in which the patterns are identical, the only difference being that the light parts of one are dark on another, and *vice versa;* but this practice was not common.

Marquetry was popular upon fine specimens of walnut veneered chests of drawers, cabinets, bureaux, tables, chairs, and mirror frames, etc., during a period of about forty years—viz., *circa* 1680–1720—the designs changing gradually the while.

Many examples of Charles II.'s reign are probably Dutch, and it is most difficult to say when the first pieces of entirely English workmanship were made, there being at this period many skilled cabinet-makers from the Low Countries regularly working here.

But, generally speaking, the more perfect construction —*e.g.*, good dovetailing in place of lapping and housing joints—stamp the native production, in addition to several fine distinctions in the marquetry design which none but the connoisseur can detect.

Another point is that English marquetry was invariably on flat surfaces in cabinet work, while the Dutch delighted in the added difficulty of laying on surfaces of concave and convex section.

As to the types of marquetry patterns. Prior to *circa* 1690 the designs generally consisted of birds and foliage in large scrolling patterns, and leaves of acanthus type in two shades of brown. During William's reign the naturalistic manner somewhat gave way to arabesque patterns, but flowers such as the jessamine with leaves remained popular in addition to bird forms, bone and ivory and holly wood being employed for petals and leaves, stained green for the latter.

About 1700 these foliage and bird forms were still in

F

evidence, but the scale of the design showed a tendency to become less; soon the flowers and then the birds were omitted, and the remaining leaves were rendered in spiky and scrolling patterns closely spaced and interwoven, the influence of the French work of Boulle often being apparent. The marquetry patterns of the early eighteenth century are frequently styled " seaweed " or " endive " (Fig. 62).

A vastly different type of marquetry is the simple geometrical sort. It generally consisted of interlacing and tangential circles of narrow lines ($\frac{1}{8}$ to $\frac{1}{4}$ inch wide) of sycamore or holly; also fan and star shapes.

With this type the " ground " was generally veneered in " oyster " wood, but other veneers, such as yew tree, plane tree, pear tree, laburnum, burr elm, etc., were employed (Fig. 70).

FIG. 58—A WALNUT CHEST UPON A STAND (*c.* 1715).

The carcase is of deal veneered in figured walnut.

The drawers are lined oak, and the fronts are edged with the early stout cock beading.

The cornice is of the small cavetto type which, with that at the top of the stand, is in cross-grain walnut.

The shaping of the stand framing is well done, and also has the cock-bead edge.

The cabriole legs are of square section, and their stiff proportions suggest a country origin.

The rear legs are straight and curiously moulded.

Height, 4 ft. 7½ in.   Width, 3 ft. 2 in.

The property of H. Avray Tipping, Esq.

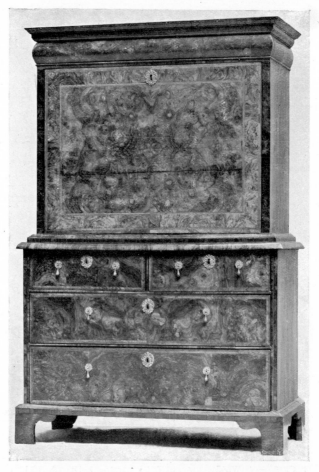

FIG. 59.—A WRITING CABINET MOUNTED UPON
A CHEST OF DRAWERS (*c.* 1705).

The whole of the front is veneered in a rich walnut of old and very irregular growth. The border strips are the feather or herring-bone pattern.

The large panel of the cabinet is hinged at the base to fall forward and has brass elbow jointed stays to support it in a horizontal position.

The architectural cornice has a large pulvenated frieze which in front is the face of a drawer. The plinth is raised on bracket feet. All mouldings are worked across the grain. The drop handles are not original.

Victoria and Albert Museum.

VII.—CABINETS

THE walnut cabinet was a most effective piece of furniture, and was another idea imported from the Continent.

In itself it consisted of a rectangular box form, generally with cornice—usually having the swell or pulvenated frieze—enclosed in front with a pair of doors, or a fall-down front to be used as a flap for writing upon.

The interior was occupied with numerous small drawers, some being secret, and possibly a small central cupboard and some open pigeon-holes.

Generally the cabinet was mounted either—

(1) Upon a stand much resembling the contemporary side tables, and of the same height. This type dates from 1675, and usually the cabinet has doors, though a fall front is not unknown (Fig. 60).

(2) Upon a chest of drawers, when it would be slightly inset in the manner of the tallboys already described (Fig. 59).

This type is most commonly found with the fall-down front, and dates from *circa* 1690, but many specimens exist with enclosing doors. The cabinet, also the frieze and drawers of the stand or the drawers, etc., of the under chest were veneered, generally in walnut, and on some specimens marquetry designs in panels and borders. All mouldings were worked across the grain, as described in the chapter on chests of drawers, etc.

The small inner drawers were built up of very thin oak, and for pulls had tiny brass knobs or drop-rings.

The fall front was hinged to the base-board of the cabinet, and was held in a horizontal position by brass elbow-jointed stays at each side.

VIII.—BOOK AND CHINA CABINETS

BOOKCASES and china cabinets with glazed doors made during the walnut period are now extremely rare.

Almost more than any other piece of furniture, the tall, glazed cabinet lent itself to the fine architectural treatment then in vogue, and following the manner of the large sash windows of the lofty rooms, the doors were divided by stout bars into well-proportioned, rectangular panes.

The cabinets were designed in two general types:

(1) The front composed of two glazed doors surmounted by a well-proportioned cornice, the interior fitted with shelves adjustable on side racks, the whole supported on a low stand after the manner of the chests of drawers upon stands already described.

(2) The upper part as No. 1, but mounted upon a broader and deeper base, fronted with low glazed doors, or containing deep drawers, and resting upon ball or bun turned feet or corner brackets (Fig. 61).

These cabinets usually had an oak carcase dovetailed at the angles and veneered with walnut. The back was of panelled oak. The doors were faced with walnut cross-banding, the mouldings and the glazing bars being in cross-grain walnut. The glass panes were frequently bevelled— a custom with the windows, as may still be seen in Wren's work at Hampton Court.

There were three phases in the design of glazing bars. The first was of a simple rounded section—similar to the half-round mould around the drawers in contemporary chests—projecting above the surface-level of the doors, and glued down to a backing strip of oak, which it overlapped on each side; it was generally formed in short, cross-grain lengths.

84

FIG. 60.—A CABINET OF SIMPLE RECTANGULAR FORM UPON A WALNUT
STAND COMPOSED OF FINE LEGS, TWIST-TURNED OVER A CARVED VASE
FORM, AND WITH FOLIATED CAPS.

*It has the veneered Y ended flat stretcher, and it is carried on ball feet.
There is a drawer in the frieze. The fall-down flap, also the sides, top, and
the interior drawers, etc., are veneered in richly figured wood—probably
laburnum—in oyster-shell patterns ; the panels are framed and banded with
lines of a darker wood which also forms the ovolo edge of the stand top.*

*It is at Ham House, and is referred to, with another very similar, in the
inventory of 1679 as a " Scriptor."*

FIG. 61.—A BOOKCASE IN OAK (*c.* 1675-80).

One of the earliest examples of this article of furniture, it is remarkable for its fine architectural character and the well-considered proportions.

The principal cupboard is well set off upon the wider under-case, to which the feeling of support is given by the panelled pilaster strips on each side.

The boldly moulded and carved sur-base avoids a sudden break and leads the eye to the large glazed doors which rise in six rows of well-proportioned panes to an excellent cornice in which a fine effect of shadow is provided by the large hollow bed mould, carved continuously with acanthus leaf. Very similar cornices are to be seen in Wren's work on screens, etc., at the Oxford and Cambridge Colleges and elsewhere.

The glazing bars are of the early type (the large astragal), but they do not project beyond the surface of the door frames as is the case with contemporary work in veneer with bar facing in cross-grain walnut.

The rounded plinth mould is unusual; the feet are of the typical bun type.

Height, 7 ft. 9 in.   Width, 4 ft. 7 in.

FIG. 62.—A WALNUT BUREAU ON STAND (*c.* 1705).

The carcase is of deal veneered in walnut with cross-banded borders.

The flap has corner reserves and quatrefoil central panel inlaid with seaweed marquetry. Two panels of similar marquetry appear on each drawer, spaces being left for the roses of the brass drop pulls.

The legs are of the inverted cup pattern, connected at the base by shaped, flat, veneered stretchers and supported upon turned ball feet.

The interior of the bureau is excellently fitted with pigeon-holes, drawers, etc., with shaped fronts and divisions.

Width, 1 ft. 10 in.   Height, 3 ft. 1½ in.   Depth, 1 ft. 3 in.

The property of Ernest Lawrence, Esq.

The second (contemporary with the first) had a square fillet added on each side, and dates from *circa* 1675. It did not rise above the door surface, and was usually in solid work; this was followed in the early mahogany and very late walnut period by a third fillet added at the apex of the curve, forming the ovolo moulded bar.

These three types, together with the developments in glazing bar design and arrangement through the eighteenth century, have been set out in diagrammatic form (p. 161).

It was usual to secure the glass with brads and putty.

Some cabinets were finely made in oak—probably by joiners rather than cabinet-makers—and polished without any veneered surface, in which cases it naturally followed that the bar work was never in cross-grained wood. The finest of this type are the bookcases in Magdalene College Library, Cambridge. The bars in these are of the second type.

Queen Mary's love of china collecting has already been mentioned, and that at least in royal palaces it was not wholly displayed on shelves and tables is proved by the fact that she employed Johnstone, the best cabinet-maker of her time, to make several cabinets for her collection of porcelain and Delft ware.*

It is very probable that reasons of construction induced the change to the bar with side and central fillets, this section having proved the strongest and most convenient in sticking—*i.e.*, running the moulding by plane—and in mitreing and tenoning at the passing joints in window work.

A few cabinets are known designed with glazed panels at their sides, but are extremely rare.

Marquetry is sometimes met with used with reserve on the fronts of glazed cabinets, but the type offered little opportunity for its employment.

* Percy Macquoid, "The Age of Walnut."

IX.—BUREAUX

THE small tables of oak and of walnut and the cabinets with fall fronts have been referred to as used for writing purposes; the latter continued in use throughout the first third of the eighteenth century. But about 1689 the bureau type made its appearance, and the first models were a utilization of the small side table and gate-leg table combined, upon which a low box was placed having a large flap at a flat angle, and containing small drawers and pigeon-holes. The flap was hinged and swung forward to be supported upon the tops of the two gate legs.

About 1695 followed the bureau on chest, in which the flap-covered compartment rested on the top of a chest of drawers with straight or shaped front, and occasionally with central knee-hole. At the base there was a projecting plinth mould and feet of the corner bracket type or turned in ball and bun forms. They ranged in width from about 2 feet 3 inches to 3 feet 6 inches. The knee-hole type was also made with flat table top, from under which a fitted writing slide could be drawn out.

The flap soon became steeper, and the space inside was more elaborately worked out in shaping the fronts and divisions of the small drawers and pigeon-holes. Also a small central cupboard was usual, treated in some architectural fashion with side pilasters, etc., behind which a secret compartment frequently was contrived.

The drawer fronts and mouldings followed the design of those on chests of drawers, the flap also being treated with veneered border strips and surrounding moulding. Marquetry was a favourite enrichment on fine specimens.

86

There was another type of very dainty bureau, about 24 inches wide, in which the box with sloping flap was mounted upon four legs of tapered and turned section, and generally with flat - shaped stretchers, veneered (Fig. 62); and from about 1705 on slender cabriole legs. These small bureaux are very scarce in walnut; they appear to date between 1690 and 1730. It was usual to veneer the entire inner surface of the flap, but some examples had a panel of green velvet.

From *circa* 1700 the bureau top became united to its supporting chest of drawers, though many retained the applied or " planted " moulding fixed around the body a few inches below the hinges of the sloping flap, which originally had covered the joint. The space within at this level was utilized as a secret well for papers, access being gained by lifting or sliding a portion of the back part of the writing surface.

There were at least two methods of supporting the flap when pulled forward into a horizontal position for writing: brass, elbow-jointed, and sliding stays were fixed at the sides; or oak bearers, running in slots just below the level of the flap hinges, could be pulled out at each side, and then acted as cantilever supports. The front ends of these bearers were faced with walnut and fitted with tiny brass knob or loop handles.

Drawers were generally oak-lined, as in the chests and cabinets, and in the small drawers of the top some very minute work is to be found, the linings often being less than $\frac{1}{8}$ inch thick, but nevertheless perfectly dovetailed. In such positions the oak has kept remarkably fresh-looking.

Beside the cleverly designed and well-made brass pulls and escutcheons, the large drawers, flaps, and doors of cabinets, etc., were fitted with specially made locks of excellent workmanship, and much skill was expended in ornamenting the keys.

X.—BUREAU BOOKCASES

THESE were bookcases mounted upon the narrow top behind the flap of the bureau, and were quite monumental in the realm of furniture. They date from the early eighteenth century. The bookcase was fitted either with adjustable shelves or with a series of pigeon-holes for books such as ledgers, and for papers, also a set of drawers, and very often a central cupboard with a cleverly treated door in prevailing architectural fashion.

There were also one or two secret compartments most cunningly contrived in what appeared to be part of the fixed construction; they operated by spring action either of wood or steel.

The bookcase had two doors, generally with arched or shaped top, and with stiles and rails veneered in cross-banded walnut, the panel of each being occupied by a Vauxhall mirror plate with bevelled edges and shaped at the top (Figs. 63 and 64).

The cornice—in cross-grain walnut—was straight, arched, or pedimented in the " broken " fashion. In the best work the backs were panelled in thin oak.

The glazing bar did not enter into the design of these pieces until later in mahogany work, when crown glass was used on the doors. At the foot of the bookcase one or two candle slides were usually fitted, consisting of thin oak trays, cross-framed at the ends and running in slots; they were faced with walnut and had small brass tray pulls (Fig. 64).

Some walnut specimens are found with veneered door panels instead of mirrors, but in many cases they are a substitution for the original glass.

88

FIG. 63.—A BUREAU CABINET IN RED LACQUER (ENGLISH WORKMANSHIP).

The hooded or arched cornice places the date at or after 1700—probably 1705. The ornament is in slight relief and finished in gold. The drawer fronts are square-edged and surrounded by the double reed mould. The doors of the cabinet are, as in the majority, filled with glass-mirror panels with shaped heads, the main curves of which rise in arch form to rhyme with the double cornice. The large cavetto mould of the cornice is also in decorated lacquer. The plinth mould is a simple cavetto, and the feet are rather tall ball shapes. The earlier pear-drop handles have now given way to a drop loop upon a shaped and engraved back place, though as yet unpierced.

Height, 6 ft. 7 in.   Width, 2 ft. 8½ in.

FIG. 64.—A BUREAU BOOKCASE VENEERED IN
WALNUT (*c.* 1720).

The fall flap of the bureau is shown open on pull-out bearers, displaying a simple arrangement of small drawers and pigeon-holes.

There is a well, reached by a movable section of the flat writing space.

The drawers display the projecting lip-moulded edges with cross-banded borders.

The bookcase is slightly inset and in its base are two slides for candles. The doors are hung on cup hinges at top and bottom, and the frames are cross-banded and retain their original Vauxhall plates with bevelled edges and shaped tops.

The cornice is finely proportioned as a broken pediment with a gilt vase on the central pedestal. Observe the fine effect obtained by the large cavetto mould on the curves of the pediment. This is shaped in deal and veneered with cross-banded walnut.

Height, 8 ft.   Width, 3 ft. 6 in.

XI.—MIRRORS

MIRRORS of glass, which for long were only within the reach of the wealthy, commenced to be made at Vauxhall, London, during the reign of Charles II.

The factory belonged to the Duke of Buckingham and others who had induced Venetian glass-makers to 'set up over here; there was at once a comparatively large demand for their products.

Records exist which show that the manufacture of glass mirrors had been carried on in England at an earlier date. In 1615 a patent was applied for by one Sir Robert Mansell to set up a factory with the help of Italians from Murano; but it is doubtful whether any English mirrors still in existence can be dated earlier than the productions of Vauxhall.

The property of reflection was obtained by the use of tinfoil coated thinly with mercury, upon which the glass was laid and subjected to pressure to obtain adhesion. This process would necessarily limit the size of the mirror; also Mr. Lenygon* states that early Vauxhall plates were limited to a length of about 45 inches owing to difficulties in grinding.

The thickness of Vauxhall plate was hardly more than half that of the modern mirror, and the bevel at the edges was so flat as to be almost imperceptible.

These mirrors were first mounted in rectangular frames made of deal, of flattish convex section, and $3\frac{1}{2}$ to $5\frac{1}{2}$ inches wide, according to the proportions of length and breadth.

. The frame was veneered in cross-banded or oyster walnut with the help of a hot caul. On fine examples marquetry was inlaid in continuous designs or in panels,

* " Furniture in England, 1660–1760."

ebony, lacquer, and tortoiseshell being also very popular for frames (Figs. 65 and 68).

These were used for the toilet also, until the small swinging mirror was introduced early in Anne's reign.

Above the broad moulded frames a fret-cut and pierced cresting was invariably fixed, frequently inlaid also; but many have been lost.

This type of mirror was of squarish proportions, and was in use throughout the reigns of William III. and Anne. About 1703 the proportion changed to a narrow and tall shape, with fairly narrow, flattish, cross-banded frame, shaped at the top, and with fret-cut cresting of more formal treatment than the earlier type. These mirrors were used as wall glasses, generally on the piers of solid wall between the tall sash windows, and it was customary to place a side table with marble top beneath them.

The frame was also formed with shaped outline, both to the glass and on the outer edge, partly veneered, and built up in solid work for carving, which was particularly rich at the foot and in the shaped and pedimented head— often widely " broken " for a central vase of flowers carved in relief. The escallop shell was popular at the base. The edge bordering the glass generally had a narrow moulding, carved and gilt.

Another type of frame for early eighteenth-century hanging mirrors was quite narrow (about $1\frac{1}{8}$ inches), of simple rounded section in cross-grain walnut, shaped at the top with S or ogee curves and arch forms, to all of which the glass was shaped and bevelled. All these mirror frames were invariably of deal construction, either lap-halved or mitred at the corners, and on the many curved parts laminated for necessary strength.

Beside the bevelled edges the mirror plates were often cut into patterns on portions of the face, or the backs were cut and engraved. In rare cases small paintings are found on the back of the glass where it is left unsilvered. On the

90

FIG. 65.—A MIRROR WITH BROAD CONVEX MOULDED
FRAME RECEDING FROM THE GLASS (*c.* 1690).

*The small inner and outer moulds are in cross-grain walnut—
as usual being built up of many short pieces. The broad ovolo is
decorated with floral design in rich marquetry.*

*The large cresting, which was invariably fitted to these mirrors
has a border of seaweed type fret-cutting, enclosing a semicircular
panel of marquetry, in which a design of flowers and foliage spread
from a circular vase—much resembling contemporary flower
painting by Dutch artists. Observe the very flat bevel on the
Vauxhall plate.*

FIG. 66.—A WALNUT TOILET MIRROR ON BOX STAND (*c.* 1702).

The glass is the original Vauxhall plate with very flat bevel, supported in shaped frame which is faced with a cross-grain walnut moulding. This is surmounted by a fret-cut cresting board. The turned supports are framed into a two-tier stand, containing four drawers at the top with one large drawer beneath, all of which are lined in very thin oak.

The carcase of the stand is deal veneered, with the drawer fronts in walnut.

Height, 2 ft. 8½ in. Width, 1 ft. 3 in. Depth of base, 7½ in.

The property of Ernest Lawrence, Esq.

long mirrors the plate was often in two pieces, there being no attempt to hide the junction, at which both were often bevelled.

The wall mirror provided scope for architectural treatment, and many frames were made either wholly or partly gilt, showing the strong influence of Wren's designs for door and window treatments — pedimented, side pilasters, enriched wide architrave, and so forth.

Such were intended for very elaborate schemes of interior decoration, and are almost beyond the scope of this book.

There was also the gesso gilt mirror in vogue at this period.

The dressing glass was a very charming introduction of the early eighteenth century; its shape was usually similar to the narrow-framed wall mirrors, and on some there is a fret-cut cresting (Fig. 66). Frequently a gilt fillet bordered the bevelled plate.

Such glasses were attached by screw-action mirror movements to a pair of plainly turned or straight, fluted, slender uprights (slightly raking backwards), which at their bases were framed into a small box constructed of deal, veneered in walnut, and fitted with several small drawers in one, two, or three tiers, which receded towards the upper tier and were often shaped in front. The drawers were oak-lined in very thin work, the fronts veneered, with various narrow borders, and fitted with brass pulls. The small feet varied, but were usually of the corner bracket type.

On some examples the set of drawers was enclosed with a slanting flap and had draw-out side bearers like a bureau in miniature; in others the sides were sloped as if to receive the flap, but the front is left open.

Another type had the mirror mounted on a bureau with slant flap (about 24 inches wide); beneath, two long drawers were generally fitted, and the whole was carried on cabriole legs of slender proportion.

91

XII.—GESSO FURNITURE

THE decoration of furniture by means of gesso must receive some notice, but comparatively small quantities were made. It was a style that could appeal only to the wealthy with rooms to spare for purely ornamental furnishings, and came in as an adjunct to the gilding of wood, the idea being to give the surfaces an all-over pattern in slight relief without the considerable expense entailed by carving it out of the solid wood. Soft woods, chiefly deal, were used, and the surface was treated with whiting and size to form a ground, upon which the same mixture was laid on thickly, following the lines of a traced pattern; when set, the forms and outlines were carefully dressed down with sharp scraping tools. Parts in strong relief were carved in wood glued to the general surface, and then thinly coated with the compo. The whole surface was finished in gilt.

This treatment was applied mostly to small tables (Fig. 67), and to mirror frames for which it was suitable and successful. The latter were usually of the pier-glass type, having leaves and scrolls in gesso on the narrow frame, and similar work on the head-piece, which was frequently capped by the " broken " pediment. This was accompanied by an extending base-board with shaped edge, carved with the escallop shell and leafage in addition to the gesso groundwork.

They were popular from about 1700 to 1735, when they appear to have gone out of fashion.

FIG. 67.—A CENTRE TABLE DECORATED WITH A SURFACE OF MOULDED
GESSO FINISHED IN GILT (*c.* 1710).

The edge of the top is ovolo moulded and curved in at the corners.

The frieze is slightly shaped and the upper part of the cabriole knee is carried round as its lowest member.

The legs are left as cut, i.e. *square in section.*

FIG. 68.—TWO VERY INTERESTING EXAMPLES
OF LACQUER FURNITURE AT HAM HOUSE.

They are mentioned in the inventory of 1679.

*The table—of the type with **S**-scroll, flat-sided legs and flat, shaped stretcher—is decorated in English lacquer of the rare incised variety. The mirror frame has a curious effect, due to the practice much in vogue at the time of cutting up the panels of imported Japanese and Chinese lacquer screens and mounting the pieces on English construction. The form of the mirror may be compared with Fig. 65.*

FIG. 69.—A TALL CUPBOARD UPON A STAND OF FIVE
LEGS WITH SHAPED STRETCHERS, FINISHED
AND DECORATED IN BLACK LACQUER.

*It dates from about 1690, and the bold arched cornice
is topped by three tiers of receding steps designed for the
display of the fashionable Chinese porcelain and Delft ware.*

*The pieces in the illustration are by no means contem-
porary, being of Staffordshire make about 100 years later.*

Height, 6 ft.   Width, 1 ft. 10 in.

FIG. 70.—A CANDLESTAND OR VASE PEDESTAL (*c.* 1685).

The top is formed as a duodecagon (twelve-sided) and has a border and five tangential circles of holly with filling of "oyster" parquetry—probably laburnum. The thumb-moulded edge is in cross-grain walnut. The top is veneered on deal. The stem is beautifully turned and together with the supports is of elm. The three supports are dovetailed into an hexagonal block, and have bun feet which have been restored.

Width of top, 12½ in.   Height, 2 ft. 8 in.

The property of the Author.

XIII.—LACQUER OF THE WALNUT PERIOD

THE rage for lacquered furniture can be attributed to the English and Dutch East India traders, who brought back screens, furniture, panels, etc., in Chinese and Japanese lacquer.

This quickly developed into a large business during the second half of the seventeenth century, and English work was also sent out " in the white " to be lacquered in the true Chinese and Japanese manner.

But the method, or rather its appearance, was copied in England to meet the demand, and was known as japanning. Actually a much more simple process than the very elaborate and perfect genuine lacquer of the East, japanning was, in its initial stages, very similar to gesso work, the ground and the portions in relief or incised being obtained by bodying up with whiting and size.

The coloured finishings were obtained by oil colours, lac varnishes, and gilding.

Many types of furniture were finished in lacquer, which was generally laid on oak construction—chests of drawers, cabinets, bureaux with and without bookcases, small tables, cabriole leg chairs and settees, wall and toilet mirrors, etc. (Figs. 63, 68, and 69).

Many fine lacquer cabinets were mounted upon richly carved stands entirely gilt or silvered.

The ground was usually black, red or blue very uncommon, and green or buff extremely rare.

Parts of the design were picked out in a variety of tints in oil colour, with gilt predominating. With the established use of mahogany, the fashion and also the amusement (for such it had become with people of leisure) began to wane, and appears to have practically ceased about 1730. It was a type of enrichment for which the village craftsman and his practical, hard-working clientele could have no use.

It was revived about the middle of the eighteenth century to meet a passing fashion among the wealthy, and then gradually changed to painted furniture.

XIV.—LONG-CASE CLOCKS

THE study of clocks is of itself a big subject, and long before the age of walnut they had been in use in one form or another.

In the walnut period interest lies in those encased in a wooden framework, and of these the first] to appear was the long-case or grandfather clock soon after the Restoration.

It is probable that the first cases to be made in England, veneered in walnut and marquetry or lacquered, appeared about the time that the first chests of drawers were so decorated, etc. — *i.e.*, *circa* 1675 – 1680 — and these were based on models imported from Holland.

Mr. Lenygon* attributes the design of the long case to the necessity of housing the " anchor " escapement invented by Dr. Hooke; also, no doubt, there was a desire to make the clock more distinctly an article of furniture, and the long case provided a good opportunity for the display of surface decoration.

Oak was invariably used for construction, and in plain clocks nothing covered this, but the fashionable examples were entirely veneered, generally in walnut, but also in yew tree, pear tree, apple tree, etc., with marquetry of various woods in addition on all fine clock cases.

There were three parts to the case: at the top the hood, covering the dial and mechanism; below this the body, enclosing the weights and pendulum; and finally the base, utilized also as a space for weight travel.

The clocks of this period constitute the early specimens, and are slender and graceful in their proportions.

* In " Furniture in England, 1660–1760."

They varied in their details of mouldings and outline, and such have been set out in comparative form on the opposite page.

From the earliest examples until *circa* 1720 the cornice of the hood was usually straight and flat-topped—occasionally with shaped and carved pediment. In the frieze a tiny fret was often applied (Fig. 71*a*).

Spiral turned columns were usually placed at the angles until *circa* 1700, but the plain turned shaft with caps and bases moulded in brass had come in about ten years prior.

The glazed hood door was square, cross-banded on the frame, or inlaid with marquetry.

The hood was broader and deeper than the body, which necessitated an important moulding at their junction, and upon the top member of this the angle columns stood (the front pair being rebated on to the sides of the hood door).

It is important to compare this moulding with that by which the body spreads out at the base. Invariably, up to about 1705, they will be found to differ considerably, but after that approximate date the trend of design was to utilize the same mould in both positions—chiefly composed of a large cavetto—which would be inverted for the base.

The front of the body consisted almost entirely of the door, which was square-headed until *circa* 1720.

A little below half its height an oval or circular hole was pierced, flanged with brass, and glazed with a " bull's-eye," generally of a greenish hue. The door had a small half-round mould fixed around and projecting over its edge in cross-grain walnut; this covered the joint with the body frame. The door and the base front were both treated together as panels, the latter having a border arranged to rhyme with the narrow width of body exposed around the door; these borders were cross-banded or filled with marquetry of small scroll patterns. The large panels were variously treated in foliage with vases, birds,

96

FIG. 71.—A CLOCK CASE IN WALNUT
VENEERS AND FLORAL MARQUETRY
(*c.* 1700), SHOWING THE NEW FASHION
OF A DOMED HOOD WITH GILDED
FINIALS.

*The marquetry on the body door is
arranged in two distinct panels with
plain veneer around the brass-rimmed
bull's-eye. The moulds at top and
bottom of the body are earlier in style
than in the other example.*

*The frame of the hood door, also the
body door and the base panel, have rich floral
designs in various woods. The border surrounding the body door and base panel is in
the later fine scrolling or seaweed type. The
frieze of the entablature has a well-designed
fret. Observe the marked difference in the
profile of the mouldings above and below the
body door, though the large cavetto in that
above the door indicates the coming change.*

*In both examples the columns flanking the
hood are plain turned, with brass caps and
bases, and the plain half-round moulding on
the edges of body doors is of the earliest type.*

THE LONG CASE CLOCK.

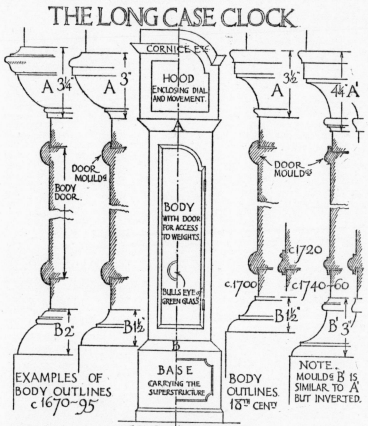

CORNICE ETC

A 3¼ A 3"

HOOD ENCLOSING DIAL AND MOVEMENT.

DOOR MOULDS

BODY DOOR.

BODY WITH DOOR FOR ACCESS TO WEIGHTS.

BULLS EYE of GREEN GLASS

B 2" B 1½"

EXAMPLES OF BODY OUTLINES. c 1670~95

BASE CARRYING THE SUPERSTRUCTURE

A 3½" 4¼ A'

DOOR MOULDS

c 1720
c 1700 c 1740~60

B 1½" B' 3"

BODY OUTLINES. 18TH CENTY

NOTE. MOULDG B' IS SIMILAR TO A' BUT INVERTED.

COMPARATIVE FEATURES.

FROM c 1670 UNTIL c 1720

CORNICE STRAIGHT; DOMED c 1695~1705
HOOD DOOR SQUARE HEADED.
BODY DOOR, SQUARE HEADED.
GLASS BULLS-EYE IN CASE DOOR.
MOULDG A DISSIMILAR FROM B
COLUMNS AT ANGLES OF HOOD, USUALLY
TWIST TURNED, c 1670 ~ c 1705.
CASE VENEERED WALNUT; MANY IN
MARQUETERIE, ALSO RED, BLACK, AND
GREEN LACQUER.   BRASS DIALS

FROM c 1740 UNTIL c 1760

CORNICE USUALLY ARCHED, NO DOME,
OFTEN A FRET CUT CRESTING & FINIALS.
HOOD & BODY DOORS ARCHED.
MOULD A SIMILAR TO B, AFTER c 1710.
COLUMNS AT ANGLES OF HOOD, TURNED
DORIC OR CORINTHIAN, BRASS CAPS &
BASES: CASE VENEERED MAHOGANY, &
IN LACQUER. BRASS & PAINTED IRON DIALS.
VERY FEW LONGCASE CLOCKS MADE IN
EARLY YEARS OF MAHOGANY PERIOD.

etc., after the Dutch manner. The marquetry patterns gradually changed, as described in cabinets, etc.

These clock cases were also made with a flattened domed hood, accompanied by brass or turned gilt finials at the two front corners and centrally on the dome (Fig. 71). They were rare prior to 1700 and after *circa* 1705.

There was a slight variation in the short plinths. The majority were solid and cross-banded, but some examples had a shaped base line with angle brackets.

The seaweed and endive marquetry soon dominated fine clock cases after 1700, but apart from that the general design was very much the same until about 1720, when the arched hood door appeared accompanied frequently by an arched body door, and some makers were already omitting the bull's-eye in the latter.

About this year the first models in mahogany were appearing, and a description of these will be found in Part III.

XV.—BEDS

AFTER the Restoration fashionable beds were almost replicas of the upholstered Italian beds imported during the first half of the seventeenth century.

Their design was now largely tempered by the prevailing architectural taste and the French influence.

The position of the bedrooms in relation to the other chief apartments must be realized in order adequately to appreciate the salient features of the late seventeenth and early eighteenth century bed.

All the principal rooms were arranged en suite on the first floor, there being through communication from room to room, as in the state apartments at Hampton Court and Kensington. The bedrooms were placed among these, as it was the prevailing fashion to hold receptions therein.

In viewing the elevation of such a house, the tallest sash windows will be found ranged and uniformly spaced to light these principal rooms, and it therefore follows that the height of the interiors would be considerable.

This was the chief cause in bringing about the slender bedposts of great height, surmounted by a richly shaped and moulded cornice. The tester was now plain, though covered with the upholstering material, which was either needlework, damask, velvet, or chintz. These materials were glued on to the surfaces of the cornice and wrapped around the posts. A shaped pelmet generally hung from the cornice edged with a rich fringe. Curtains were hung at the four corners, and were continued across the head of the bed.

Many were quite fantastic in their gorgeous colourings and plumed cornices—far too expensive and quite unsuitable for the smaller houses, where the quiet contentment born of hard work and simple living still tolerated the oak bed of two generations back.

FIG. 72.—BRASS MOUNTS IN USE FROM THE RESTORATION
TO *temp.* GEORGE II.

The acorn and pear-drop drawer pulls were in general use c. 1660–1700. *They are in cast brass.*

The shaped back plates are cut out with bevelled edges and in many cases are engraved on the face. These gave way to pierced designs from c. 1720.

The drop loops are of cast brass, held by iron or brass wire until c. 1700, *after which date the best handles had loops swinging from the knob heads of fixing bolts, on which the screw thread appears.*

Where the plates were intended for keyhole scutcheons they were fixed with brass tacks. ·

The shaped hinges were used for cupboard doors.

Part III

THE PERIOD OF MAHOGANY FURNITURE

(Circa 1715 to Early Nineteenth Century)

I.—HISTORICAL NOTE

THE first year of the reign of George I. may be taken as a convenient but approximate date in which furniture began to appear in mahogany.

The new wood came into use as a fashionable and expensive novelty, practically unknown and unheeded by any save the nobility, who still remained staunch patrons of the arts without Court leadership.

The new king was a Hanoverian, and took no interest in the arts and crafts of England.

The early mahogany period was essentially one of transition. Walnut wood, though approaching the end of its course, was still fashionable in the bedrooms of the nobility, whilst in the provinces it was in constant and general demand in the homes of the country gentlemen and well-to-do farmers. Therefore the new intruder did little damage to the home-grown timber trade until the middle of the century.

It is known, however, that but few walnut trees were planted after 1700, and it was not until the latter years of the Napoleonic wars, *circa* 1810–1815, that the tree again received the arboriculturist's attention, when numbers were planted to replace the great amount used in making rifle butts.

The simple solid furniture of the labouring classes was still being made by village carpenters and joiners in English oak, and in this material the plainer designs in the changing styles throughout the eighteenth century were reproduced—naïvely, but with peculiar charm.

In addition to this use of oak, it was still in considerable

103

demand by the great London cabinet-makers for drawer linings and certain constructional framings. For carcase work, the experience gained during the walnut period compelled the retention of the finest quality oak and deal upon which to lay the veneers of mahogany, satinwood, and various inlays, though in certain cases mahogany was used for the purpose; and in the second half of the century a red fir or pine became more popular than the yellow deal.

In regard to the early use of mahogany, the history of walnut at the Restoration was repeated; from 1715 to 1725 or thereabouts it was used almost entirely in solid work in manufacturing chairs, stools, chair-back settees, card tables, etc., all of which differed but little from the late walnut models of Queen Anne's reign.

In sorting out the types of early mahogany furniture, it appears that the reception and dining rooms and the hall were the first to be refurnished in the now fashionable wood; while walnut veneered chests of drawers, cabinets, bureaux, etc., were still being made and retained in bedrooms and the smaller private apartments. It is probable, however, that walnut would have gone out of favour entirely in fashionable circles when mahogany commenced being imported in regular shipments had it not been for the heavy tax levied upon all imported timber. This fact undoubtedly gave an extra lease of life to English walnut by considerably adding to the selling price of mahogany furniture, which wood, by the very nature of its substance, proved costly in labour time.

This tax was entirely removed in 1747.

In the Introduction I referred to the important part which architects were to play in the later history of English furniture. This time had now arrived.

Sir Christopher Wren and his craftsmen, in the superb handling of many fine works, exercised an enormous influence which extended well into the eighteenth century, and was the basis of design of a large amount of important furniture.

The nobility were taking an ever-growing interest in architecture and decoration, vying with one another in the erection of stately mansions, and consulting their architects on all matters relevant to the complete furnishing and equipment of the whole house; these people of wealth and leisure were constantly travelling, chiefly to Italy, collecting marbles and other fragments of the ancient Roman Empire; and with the help of draughtsmen accompanying them, they returned with measured drawings of many of the classic ruins and Renaissance palaces of Italy, upon which the elevations of their prospective houses frequently were based. One notable case was the Earl of Burlington and his architect, William Kent, whom he probably met in Italy.

Kent became notorious, not alone as society architect and designer of furniture, but in the absurd craze of the time was regarded as a veritable compendium of artistic knowledge and taste, even to the extent of being consulted by ladies about their dresses.

As to Kent's ability in the "mistress art" it is not our purpose here to enquire; in furniture he was no less ambitious, though certainly not so successful. His opportunity was a great one; questions of expense were never present to curb his hand, yet his work is generally ponderous and ungainly, indicating little appreciation of the essentials in furniture design or the lines and proportions that make for beauty.

One point, however, he grasped thoroughly, and that was scale. His furniture was designed to complete the scheme of decoration of great apartments, chiefly the state rooms of noblemen's mansions, and the mixture of architectural motifs incorporated in his pieces was quite in sympathy with his handling of the walls, doorways, windows, and fireplaces. The nobility alone were patrons of this specially designed and very expensive architect's furniture; the trade paid no heed to it, and continued to work on a natural development of the simple fashions approved and accepted by all in Queen Anne's reign.

There are several characteristics by which the architect's furniture of the early mahogany period can easily be recognized.

It shows in a great many instances an inability to gain the " feeling " of furniture proper as distinct from the architectural woodwork fixed in the rooms.

Naturally it embodies many features of the classic style then considered necessary to important compositions; consequently the fronts of bookcases, cabinets, etc., were designed in heavy and dignified manner, following the accepted proportions for masonry structures, having attached columns or pilasters surmounted with an entablature, and often with pediment in addition—a complete essay in an order of Roman architecture.

This heavy furniture rapidly went out of fashion after 1740, and was as rapidly replaced by the contemporary fashions reigning in France, which quickly produced lightness of design largely divorced from architectural influence. The fine qualities of mahogany led to daring feats in construction, which resulted in a gaiety of effect unknown in Queen Anne walnut.

It is important to realize that the designing of furniture was now approached with more preliminary care and thought than in the work of the seventeenth century and earlier. In the old English oak, the general dimensions having been settled, the various parts were set out direct upon the prepared wood, and the decoration roughly marked on and worked either before or after construction. In the walnut period also this obtained to some extent, the craftsman basing his designs on foreign models.

But with the early eighteenth century the designs began to be worked out in detail on paper, in which the proportions of mass and mouldings could be carefully considered and settled with precision. The carving would also be made the subject of a full-size cartoon, and in very important work models were actually made.

Infinitely more successful as a furniture designer than Kent or his contemporaries was Robert Adam, who, with his brother James, were the leading English architects between 1760 and 1792. On several occasions he commissioned the Chippendale firm to make furniture from his drawings, and much of this very excellent work remains to this day in the rooms for which it was originally designed.

In giving a very large part of his time to considerations of decoration and furniture Robert Adam was undertaking no more than that usually required of an eighteenth-century architect. In all important commissions in those days the construction of the actual building was regarded as the first part of a comprehensive scheme—the shell which would house the decorations and furniture and everything necessary to render the building complete and ready for occupation.

Needless to say, this involved consideration of a host of minute detail on the part of the architect, but, on the other hand, it gave him the opportunity to impart a perfect sense of balance and harmony, and prevented the introduction of furnishings which, in the hands of others, might easily have led to the destruction of those very ideals which he had in mind when designing the actual building.

In the case of Robert Adam these allied arts were interpreted with masterly skill. His training and his studies in Italy and Dalmatia were the basis of his style, which, though drawn from the monumental work of the ancients—the same old stuff that Hawksmoor, Vanburgh, Kent, and Gibbs had used with heavy hand—was cleverly recast and so adapted, as to appear with a new meaning.

107

Purity and grace of line and form, with delicate application of refined detail, constituted the charm of Robert Adam's designs. They were at once accepted as something really great and eminently suitable to domestic architecture of the larger sort.

The effect on other of the crafts was remarkable. The silversmiths and Sheffield plate-makers adopted the new shapes and enrichments, as also did Josiah Wedgwood in his fine services of Queen's Ware.

And in furniture Adam's designs were very largely assumed by Hepplewhite and many other firms of contemporary date.

In the popular mind the work of the mahogany period is summed up as the work either of Chippendale, Hepplewhite, or Sheraton, but these time-honoured names can only be used as generic titles to certain styles of work, the great mass of which cannot possibly have emanated from their workshops, though in many cases no doubt from their designs.

A small quantity of fine furniture can be traced to the Chippendale firm—none with certainty to Thomas Chippendale's own hand.

Nothing extant can be positively assigned to George Hepplewhite or the firm of A. Hepplewhite* and Co., which was formed after his death in 1786.

And of "Sheraton" furniture the same applies, it being even doubtful whether Thomas Sheraton actually "made" as a practical craftsman after coming to London in 1790.

The eighteenth century was remarkable for the large number of books published by members of the building, decorating, and furnishing trades. About forty were published between 1739 and 1816, the best known being Chippendale's "The Gentleman's and Cabinet-maker's Director," 1754, with two further editions 1759 and 1762; Hepplewhite's "The Cabinet-maker's and Upholsterer's

* Alice Hepplewhite, his widow.

Guide," 1788, with two further editions 1789 and 1794; and Thomas Sheraton's "Cabinet-maker's and Upholsterer's Drawing Book," 1791, with subsequent edition in 1793–94; and in 1803 his "The Cabinet Dictionary." The Society of Upholsterers and Cabinet-makers, Lock, Mainwaring, Ince and Mayhew, Edwardes and Darly, Crunden, Chambers (the architect), and others, also contributed to the subject.

These, with the possible exception of Sheraton's books, were really trade lists, illustrated with designs likely to interest wealthy patrons. They indicate the appreciation of advertisement and the laborious means of carrying it into effect in those days.

It will thus be seen that the designs which Chippendale, for instance, showed in his "Director," would reach every cabinet-maker in the country who cared to invest in a copy of the book, and would be accepted as models of fashionable London work to be made up according to the degree of skill of the individual craftsman. This accounts very largely, not only for the country-made "Chippendale" furniture of varying quality, but also for much that was made from designs in the various trade catalogues then in circulation.

The perusal of these books leaves the reader rather cold, the numerous line engravings being most uninspiring, and many of them are vulgar in their excess of ornament; the perspective is distinctly humorous.

Very little is known regarding the most renowned of cabinet-makers—Thomas Chippendale. It is established that he came to London with his father some time about 1727. The older man had worked at Worcester, principally as a carver and gilder of picture frames, and no doubt resumed this business in London with the son's assistance, the latter building up a connection in chair and cabinet making. In 1749 Chippendale II. took a shop off Long Acre, but during the twenty-two years that had elapsed since his arrival in London he must have executed a large amount of work, not in what is termed the Chippendale style, but in the early Georgian fashions. It is the work of this period which came from his own hand—never to be recognized.

A little later, when he removed to better premises in St. Martin's Lane and published his noted "Director," he employed many craftsmen, and, as head of a large and flourishing concern, it is probable he no longer worked at the bench, except at times on a little special carving perhaps.

At his death in 1779 the business was carried on by his son (the third Chippendale), who had as partner Haig, one of his father's employees; and it should be remembered that this firm continued producing furniture until the early years of the nineteenth century, not in the style by which its reputation had been made, but following the changing fashions of the so-called Hepplewhite, Sheraton, and Empire styles.*

The earlier work upon which Chippendale evolved his mature designs was in form based on the natural developments of the walnut fashions, enriched with superb carving, at first classical, then becoming decidedly French in character. He could not, however, afford to ignore the craze for reviving Gothic detail which had been growing amongst the nobility for some years. Also, due to the continued trade with the East, there was an important revival of the Chinese taste. In neither of these passing fashions were the originals properly understood, and many very absurd productions naturally resulted; but in justice to Chippendale, Ince and Mayhew, Lock, and a few other firms, it must be admitted that they grafted Gothic and Chinese motifs on to their mahogany with rare skill, though they were wont to mix in a little French detail to give it a relish.

* See the bedroom suite made by Chippendale and Haig for David Garrick at the Victoria and Albert Museum.

The designs of the brothers Robert and James Adam completely changed the public taste, and from about 1765 they began to influence furniture. This now took on a still lighter and more dainty treatment, the majority of it classical, but extremely graceful and suitable, and quite unlike the ponderous classicism of Kent. Much also was French in feeling, but " Adamized " into truly English furniture.

It was in this manner that such firms as Hepplewhite, Shearer, Seddon, Sons and Shackleton, and Gillow worked, though some of their designs mark an appreciation of Chippendale II.'s productions, and a regard for French work of a slightly earlier date.

Once again furniture was becoming gay with colour ; the true mahogany period was giving way about 1765 before a new taste for lighter woods—chiefly satinwood— which were polished without staining, and in addition to inlays, portions of the surfaces were painted in subjects, floral sprays and swags, for which, on some of the best work, such renowned artists as Angelica Kaufmann, Cipriani, and others were employed.

Painted decoration was largely out of fashion by 1790, when the vogue of inlay again came to the fore; this also was associated with very dainty forms, and the colour was varied by staining portions of the inlay and in using a great variety of boldly figured foreign woods cut in veneer. Many tea caddies, knife boxes, and urns show this manner to perfection.

Such work is popularly known as Sheraton, and he certainly did much to improve the style. His many designs show distinct refinement and purity of form, though somewhat at the risk of necessary strength.

Quite a large amount of simple mahogany furniture was constructed during the years of composite style which mark the last two decades of the eighteenth century and the early years of the nineteenth, but some of the

111

canons of craftsmanship were being cast down, tentatively at first, in response to the demand for cheap yet good-looking furniture. This arose from the new middle classes, who were largely composed of the trading section of the community.

Consequently, some of the original intentions were often set aside. For instance, the true purpose of veneering had always been to obtain variety of tone by showing the very beautiful figure in the wood, which could only be got by cutting in certain directions, often quite contrary to the grain; but in these later years the very plainest Honduras mahogany was cut in veneers also and laid upon pine for facing chests of drawers, bureaux, etc., which thus gave the appearance of plain solid Honduras, yet could be sold at a substantially lower figure.

This and the accompanying decline in originality of thought were the beginning of the end. With the opening of the nineteenth century the Sheraton style was losing in interest and becoming absurd. There was a certain liveliness in the passing craze for " Empire " designs commencing about 1805, but they lacked the vitality of all the earlier work.

As with architecture, the dependent and allied arts were falling upon very lean years; all inspiration seemed lacking, and traditional craftsmanship was losing its hold. Commercialism was soon to carry all before it, and with the advance of the Victorian era many of the ancient handicrafts of England had all but ceased to live.

The mahogany of the eighteenth century and that generally used to-day are very different materials.

The first mahogany to be imported was the so-called " Spanish," brought from the island of San Domingo, lying to the east of Cuba; the early Spanish explorers had named this island Espanola, which apparently is the reason for the name given to the wood. Here forests

adjacent to the coast contained fine timber of great age.*
Very similar was the mahogany obtained from the neigh-
bouring islands of Cuba, Puerto Rico, and Jamaica, on
which the high rocky soil had produced trees of very slow
growth, which in consequence were intensely close in the
grain. The wood was dark and rich in colour, the San
Domingo having very little figure, while that from the
other islands was often better marked. When seasoned,
such wood proved most laborious to work, and necessitated
tools of the best quality steel, very frequently sharpened
to great keenness. This hard mahogany actually acquires
a polish simply by the process of planing the surface.

Carving executed in Spanish mahogany exhibits a
crispness comparable with chased metal, and has so remained to this day on many fine pieces.

The density of this wood gave its own characteristics
to the old work, and no better illustration can be given than
the marvellous pierced and carved splat work on the back
of chairs *circa* 1745–1760. It was like working in a metal
that was possible of hand manipulation; the skilled work-
man was able to cut his mortices and tenons with such
accuracy that when fitting them together the air was all
but imprisoned in the cavity, and finally escaped with an
audible rush.

Towards the middle of the century there was a large
demand for mahogany chests of drawers, cabinets, bookcases, etc., bringing into play the old art of veneering;
few such pieces had been required in the earlier years of
the period owing to the retention of walnut furniture of
these types.

Cuban wood was mostly cut for veneers, and several
varieties of remarkably beautiful figure were obtained,
known as " clouded," " fiddle-back," " curl," etc.†

* Like the finest English oak, maturity was not reached until
about 200 years of growth.
† The finest figured veneers were not employed until after 1750.

H   113

Another mahogany was imported in the second half of the eighteenth century, obtained from forests on the coast of Honduras in Central America; it was also known as baywood. It is a tree of quicker growth, and is much lighter in weight and colour; the grain is open and straight, and the wood is easy to work. It shrinks extremely little, and when used was generally stained. Due to the nature of the grain, the old methods of polishing took very much longer than was required when working in " Spanish " or Cuban.

Regarding veneering, the finest red pine was usually the base for this work, and the veneer was laid in larger pieces than had been general in walnut. A whole panel, for instance, would be faced with one sheet of veneer, displaying magnificent curl figure, the flash in the grain being finest up the centre and dying off on each side to a wonderful depth of tone; panels were often halved and quartered. The feather or herring-bone borders were no longer attempted, and cross-banding was not very general before 1765, after which, in addition to its familiar use as a narrow border, it was also employed in facing the frames of glazed doors and on panels when forming the surround of a centrally placed oval of vertical figure edged with holly or box lines; this late cross-banding is always mitred at the corners, which is a distinct improvement on many walnut specimens where it was square butted.

Inlay did not appear until Robert Adam adopted it in border patterns and marquetry panels of classical subjects, some fine specimens being made from his designs by Chippendale about 1760, after which date it continued popular, though becoming less formal, on many of the best Hepplewhite and Sheraton style pieces.

Another very important distinction between walnut and mahogany furniture concerned the mouldings; the method with the former of building up in cross-grain sections on a deal backing was discarded in favour of mouldings run with the grain (by a moulding plane before they were fixed) and fixed by glue and panel pins.

Only were they built up of short lengths when working around quick curves, such as the cornices of bow-fronted corner cupboards.

Small mouldings were bent to curves—by steaming first if necessary.

Mouldings in mahogany were frequently carved up till about 1775.

Satinwood in the solid and as veneer or inlay enjoyed a great vogue, from *circa* 1770 to 1795 much fashionable furniture being constructed in or faced with this East Indian importation, to the partial exclusion of mahogany for lightly designed chairs, settees, card and occasional tables, cabinets, etc.; it was polished without staining to enhance its own light yellow tones. It was soon discovered that certain cuts of chestnut veneers would give a very similar effect, and birch, coloured up, was also used to simulate satinwood for tapering legs, etc.

Many other woods were employed in veneering panels and borders.

Those of native growth were pollarded walnut, oak, and elm; the burrs of walnut and elm; sycamore, chestnut, box, yew, holly, harewood (dyed sycamore), beech, pear, cherry, and laburnum.

Beside satinwood, those imported were tulipwood, kingwood, amboyna, thuya, rosewood, zebrawood, snakewood, etc. Thin tortoiseshell was also used as a veneer. The surface finishing varied according to the article and the type of wood.

Some pieces made of the hardest Spanish mahogany were left untouched by varnish, oil, or wax. Others were treated with poppy or linseed oil, or were beeswaxed, it being a comparatively easy matter to obtain a fine polish on the hardest varieties.

When Honduras wood was employed, the more open

and softer grain needed a longer process. One laborious method, but productive of excellent results, was to use powdered brickdust with linseed oil under a pad, which by continual rubbing resulted in a fine hard-wearing polish. Frequently the oil was dyed with alkanet root. When beeswax was used, the surfaces were usually first treated with two or three coats of gum lac dissolved in spirit, which sank into and filled the grain, so making it easier to get a rich polish with the wax. In using the wax on chairs and over carving, it was applied with a rather stiff brush and also polished with a brush.

French polishing was not then understood,* and without question this modern method of polishing is inferior to the old, both as regards appearance and durability.

A very fine quality varnish was used by the best cabinet-makers of the eighteenth century; several coats were applied at intervals, and a polish of exquisite softness was finally obtained by rubbing the surfaces with rotten-stone and oil solely with the palm of the hand.

The brass handles, drawer pulls, and escutcheons of the mahogany period underwent many changes. From 1715 to 1735 the slender drop loop on a shaped back plate, either pierced or solid, was retained (Figs. 72 and 129), as during these years the greater part of the furniture containing drawers was still made in walnut.

About 1740 a great modification set in. The drop loop became stouter and was shaped like a bird's beak against each bolt head, behind which was a plainly moulded circular rose instead of the linking back plate (Fig. 129). This type remained throughout the century, being much

* Mr. Cescinsky considers it could not have been known in this country before 1820 (" English Furniture of the 18th Century," Vol. III.). Sheraton's " Cabinet Dictionary " of 1803 gives several old methods then in use.

enriched for some of Adam's fine pieces. After 1750 brass pulls and escutcheons began to be made for the French market in cast and chased metal in the Messonnier style, and such were used on commodes, chests of drawers, etc., of English make designed with strong French characteristics. Varieties of these rococo forms were popular until the Adam régime, when simplicity of form again became dominant, and the back plate returned, agreeing with the carved or inlaid circular and oval rosettes and pateræ.

In 1777 a Birmingham brassfounder, John Marston, improved upon a process of stamping brass goods invented in 1769, and applied it successfully to furniture fittings.* After this date the back plates of drawer pulls—of oval, circular, and octagonal outline—were ornamented and moulded by stamping thin sheet brass so that it appeared hollow at the back (Fig. 129).

This was contemporary with the stamping of thin silver for the enrichments and mounts of Sheffield plate. Other late types were knob shapes having a stamped face, such as a wreath of flowers, a lion's head, etc., and fitted with a screw or bolt for securing to the wood.

The turned mahogany knob appeared about 1800, either fitted with a brass screw or the knob was set in a stamped brass cup to which a bolt was attached. The mahogany knobs with wood screws found on many drawers are Victorian substitutions.

* Victoria and Albert Museum Handbook on Catalogues of the Metal Trades.

11.—CHAIRS

THE earliest specimens of mahogany chairs—*i.e.*, those made from about 1715 to 1720, and in many cases later—are indistinguishable from the late Queen Anne fashions, and are dissimilar only in their deep colour and absence of veneering, both woods being used concurrently on the best work until *circa* 1730.

These early specimens of mahogany chairs may be regarded as the test pieces of a new material; in working on them the craftsman acquired a practical insight into mahogany characteristics which, once grasped, enabled him to evolve a treatment of design peculiar and proper to the finest known wood for furniture construction.

For many years there was no attempt to banish the cabriole leg; the plain, beautifully balanced type, with club foot, that had proved so satisfactory in walnut, was retained in mahogany on the simpler designs until after 1750.

For the finer specimens, the foot was carved as a bird's claw and ball, or as a lion's claw, and from about 1725 to 1740 the knee was often finely carved in the prevailing classic architectural manner with the lion or satyr mask, or the shell and husk. The projecting horizontal members of the arms were similarly carved with heads (Fig. 73).

The earlier solid splat was quickly discarded for one of open design; the piercing was very plain at first—a series of narrow vertical cuts, leaving about five slender uprights grouped in the centre. This splat was framed into the shoe on the top of the back seat rail and into the under side of the top rail, which, though still shaped, was

118

FIG. 73.—AN UPHOLSTERED ARMCHAIR IN MAHOGANY (*c.* 1730).

The seat and back are covered with the original needlework.

The arms are carved with lion heads, then greatly in fashion. Many chairs had the lion mask on the knee with which the claw foot is a suitable finish ; in this instance the earlier shell and husk is carved on the knee of the cabriole leg.

The property of Percival D. Griffiths, Esq.

FIG. 74.—AN EARLY CHAIR OF THE MAHOGANY
PERIOD (*c.* 1730).

*The front legs shaped in plain cabriole form, the rear legs in
slight cabriole profile with club feet. The uprights are devoid of
the break above the seat frame and continue in a slight outward
curve to the horizontal top rail. The splat is very simply pierced
and rises from a scrolled shoe; each bar of the splat is, in this case,
a separate member. The seat frame is sufficiently deep to permit
of a band, carved with the Vetruvian scroll, beneath the stuffed-
over seat. This band was usually applied over a beech frame.*

becoming less arched or hooped, and squarer at the corner junctions with the back uprights (Fig. 74).

With ever-increasing skill and inventiveness of design the splat became daringly pierced, and often richly carved in a wonderful variety of patterns according to the vogue of the moment, though in many cases the outline is reminiscent of the solid vase and fiddle-shaped walnut splats (Fig. 75).

This process of costly splat enrichment took place between 1740 and 1765, and included all the designs in French, Gothic, and Chinese taste. After the latter date the designs of Robert Adam and others greatly modified the chair back.

The hoop back of Queen Anne chairs was not entirely dropped, but in the majority the uprights were devoid of the break just above the seat frame, and continued with a gradual outward curve to the top rail, where the back was widest.

Below the seat frame the rear legs gradually converged to the floor; viewed sideways, the complete outline of legs with the uprights shows the extremities well to the rear of the seat frame.

This involved a rather complicated setting out in shaping those members, and required accurate templates for both faces in addition to a large piece of mahogany.

From about 1735 to 1740 the bold, heavy classicism of Kent's style was going out of favour before the new taste for the fantastic French rococo ornament. This was very suitable for chairs, being low in relief and not detracting from the main lines of the design when used appropriately. In English work it was quite new, and after 1750 became so profuse as to give the chairs a rather un-English character. Chippendale, in illustrating such chairs, quite fearlessly describes them as French, which makes it pretty clear that in and about 1754 French designs were quite in the fashion.

The most important types of Kent's chairs were

upholstered in rich velvets and damasks, the seat being stuffed over and the backs stuffed in, with uprights and top rail of low, heavy proportions, exposed and richly carved. Frequently the legs were of a cumbersome scroll shape with flat side faces, on which the scale pattern was carved. The legs were placed in position similarly to the cabriole type; the face of the leg was carved with leafage, shells, or masks, and in some instances carved swags of fruit and flowers were arranged between the legs on front and side.

On some chairs Kent adopted the square tapering leg with moulded plinth; in such cases the arm supports rise from the front corners and curve backwards as they rise to the horizontal arms. It should be noted that this taper leg was revived by Adam about 1765, much reduced in mass, and the receding arm support reappeared from about 1755, also more delicately rendered.

The seat frame, usually very deep and exposed beneath the material, was carved with formal classic detail, the great favourite being the wave or Vitruvian scroll (Fig. 74). Another was the key ornament.

Naturally Kent could not ignore the cabriole leg, to which he often added the French whorl or scroll foot about 1740. Some he utterly spoilt by carving of unsuitable classic ornament; on others he was content to retain the club or claw and ball foot, with acanthus leafage scrolling from the shoulder-pieces and gracefully sweeping over the knee, but in such cases he was following the work of contemporary chair-makers rather than his own feeling for design.

The chairs with square or cabriole legs were invariably either of walnut or mahogany, upon which the enrichment was occasionally gilded. Those of more pretentious design, with bolder carving and scroll legs, were generally of soft wood with surfaces prepared in size and whiting and gilt entirely.

FIG. 75.—AN ARMCHAIR IN MAHOGANY (c. 1745).

The cabriole legs are carved on the knees with classic type acanthus, and the feet are carved with the claw and ball. The rear legs retain the club-footed form of Queen Anne models.

The back uprights show the double curvature which was retained until c. 1760. The top rail also is of the form used by Chippendale and many others. The splat is of well-developed form and piercing but remains perfectly flush on the face; it rises from the typical shoe piece. The serpentine arms project and scroll over the curved supports, which are secured to the side rails of the seat. The seat frame is moulded on the top edge and rebated for a drop-in seat.

FIG. 76 —AN ARMCHAIR IN MAHOGANY (*c.* 1760).

The back uprights and arm supports moulded. The top rail of the back is edged with narrow C *scrolls combined with leaf carving. The splat is of vase outline, pierced to form interlacing loops, with a suggestion of Gothic shapes; here again the* C *scroll and leaf edging appear. The square legs and stretchers are typical. The seat is serpentine in front and stuffed over.*

The property of Stanley J. May, Esq.

The rather stiff acanthus carving on the cabriole knees was practically the only classic motif which survived after 1740, and provided a convenient via media for the grafting on of French ornament which now was rising rapidly to favour. The latter was also adapted from the acanthus, but was more scroll-like in its form, and the leaf spikes were always finished in a peculiar twist.

The acanthus and its variations were now employed to enrich all parts of the open-work back in addition to the knees of the legs; this carving was executed with great skill, and was varied in scale exactly to harmonize with the proportions of the construction upon which it was cut in delicate relief.

The splat was often pierced to represent a balanced group of C scrolls and flat strap work cleverly interlaced. In some early examples the splat was left solid in the upper half, of scrolling outline, and edged with acanthus leafage carved out of a raised piece after gluing on to the splat.

The two general types of arms used on late walnut chairs were still popular, the shaped supports rising from the side rails of the seat frame a few inches behind the front corners.

From about 1745 to 1760 the plainer sets of mahogany chairs retained the simple strap work and C-scroll splats, with possibly a little rococo ornament on the faces and the shaped top rail. With such the legs were good plain cabriole shapes until *circa* 1755, the seat either on a separate drop-in frame or stuffed over and often serpentine in front. About 1755, in accordance with a new fashion, the less expensive straight square leg came in, but did not entirely supersede the cabriole (Fig. 76).

By 1745 the full style of the French rococo was in great demand for fashionable furniture, and very costly chairs were made in the finest San Domingo and Cuban wood, profusely carved on the legs, arms, back frame, and splat.

121

On such chairs the cabriole leg was sometimes carved with simple mouldings accentuating its vertical curvature, and these were broken in places by excrescences of small leaf scrolls, which were also worked in great variety on the shoulder-pieces and frequently carried across the seat frame on a wavy scroll outline.

Very important amongst the ornament derived from French work was the cabochon—appearing like a small cartouche on the knee of the cabriole and surrounded by typical leaf carving. In some specimens this motif was also embodied on the top rail of the back.

The pierced splat was also enriched with the ribbon treatment, which was skilfully embodied with scrolls and eaf carving. The curves were also arranged to sweep up into the lines of the top rail, and so appear to be all cut from a single plank of mahogany; careful inspection, however, will reveal the perfect jointing.

These apparently most delicate splats are remarkably strong, the effect of lightness being obtained largely by cutting back the return faces of each member so that they are narrower at the back. The piercings were cut out with a fret-saw and the rear arrises trimmed off with a chisel; when this was done the tool marks are apparent, and form a striking contrast to the immaculate finish of the front of the splat.

In certain examples the splat was designed to unite with the side uprights in some sort of ribbon motif, but is seldom successful.

The types of seat frame shaping developed in the walnut chairs continued in use so long as the cabriole leg was employed, but with the adoption of the square leg, *circa* 1755, the corners were always square, the sides still tapered to the back, and the front was straight or serpentine (Figs. 76 and 77).

The cabriole leg greatly declined in favour after the publication of Chippendale's " Director " in 1754, but was

122

(a)   (b)

FIG. 77.—(a) MAHOGANY CHAIR (c. 1760-65).

The seat is slightly serpentine and stuffed over. The legs are square, connected with four plain stretchers. The back uprights are moulded, and the top rail illustrates a "rounded" type. The splat is rather open, consisting of piercings based on Gothic forms with acanthus carved on the solid. The serpentine arms do not project beyond their supports, which in itself is good evidence of late date.

(b) A MAHOGANY CHAIR (c. 1760) WITH SEAT, LEGS, ETC., AS (a).

The splat is delicately cut with Gothic forms and details out of one piece.

The property of Messrs. Wm. Morris & Co.

FIG. 78.—AN UPHOLSTERED ARMCHAIR IN MAHOGANY
(*c.* 1760).

*The interlaced strapwork carved on the legs and arm supports,
together with the shaped brackets, indicates the Chinese taste
which largely affected fashionable furniture after* 1755.

*The padded arms are very short, due to the bold backward sweep
of their supports, which are framed to the seat rail above the front
legs.*

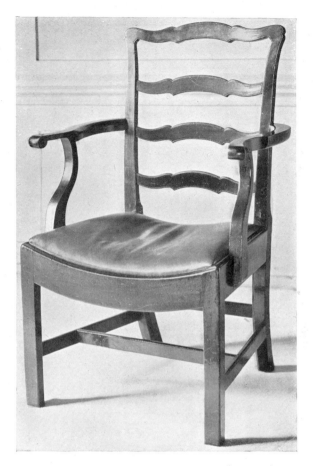

FIG. 79.—A MAHOGANY ARMCHAIR (*c.* 1770).

Probably country made. This is a simple example of the type with ladder rails, which in this case are shaped but not pierced. Very valuable to the design is the tiny scratched bead edging the back uprights and rails. The arms continue the earlier manner by projecting beyond the supports. The seat has a dipped framing—a feature rare before 1768. *The legs and stretchers retain the solidity which was now giving way before the lighter style of Robert Adam.*

The property of Edward Hudson, Esq.

FIG. 80.—A WRITING CHAIR IN WALNUT (*c.* 1755).

The legs are square with the inner edge chamfered off; the outer edge is softened with a small bead, which is also worked along the seat rails.

The seat is square on a drop-in frame. Three of the legs are carried up to support a semicircular top rail, which is surmounted by a shaped and moulded block.

The two splats rise from the typical shoe-pieces; they are well cut and carved in slight relief.

The property of Stanley J. May, Esq.

again adopted in a slender form on French type chairs during the ensuing Adam period.

About 1750 the Gothic taste developed in furniture. Feeble reproductions of mediæval building forms and ornament had been a vogue with the nobility for about thirty-five years ; many gardens had been laid out embodying structures such as mock ruins, which their authors called Gothic. Then, in 1747, the Gothicizing of Strawberry Hill, Twickenham, was commenced by Sir Horace Walpole. The chair-makers rose to the occasion and changed their French style to mediæval English. The early specimens (*circa* 1750) had the cabriole leg with claw and ball foot—nothing Gothic about that—but the splat was pierced with designs of tracery, ogee arches, crockets and cusps, very well composed and adapted to a chair back.

The straight square leg came in about 1754, and was more in keeping with the Gothic splat, but a little French ornament was frequently incorporated, particularly on the top rail and the arms. Also about this date the stretchers reappeared. For their reintroduction there is no satisfactory explanation; on structural grounds they had for long been considered superfluous, yet suddenly they reappeared on chairs of Gothic taste and between cabriole as well as the square legs. They were of simple rectangular section, about $\frac{5}{8}$ inch wide and $1\frac{1}{4}$ inches deep, and with the general use of the square leg the stretchers were always present, whatever style might be exhibited in the design of the back, but those on Gothic chairs were frequently widely chamfered with stops to leave a normal section at the joints.

The Chinese taste was the rage of another distinguished group of art patrons, among whom the work of China and Japan was regarded as eminently suitable to English decoration and furniture, leaving to the craftsmen the many awkward details involved in adapting Eastern forms to English construction. Fortunately, mahogany

123

happened to be the wood in general use, and probably alone capable of being cut into intricate pierced frets and trellis designs without warping or snapping on the short grain. About 1757 the architect Sir William Chambers,* having returned from a voyage to China, published a book, " Designs in the Chinese Taste," which offered many suggestions alike to the patron and cabinet-maker, and undoubtedly had considerable influence.

The dominating lines of the " Chinese " chairs were the vertical, horizontal, and diagonal bars of the pierced trellis with which the back was filled, and also the spaces enclosed by the straight horizontal arms and their supports. On some particularly rich examples the top rail was shaped and carved to represent a pagoda roof, and the trellis panel was very rich in its fencing and arched bar work. The arm panels invariably leant outward at a decided angle, which necessitated an inward curve at the rear of the arm itself in order to meet and frame into the side of the back upright.

The legs were generally square, the front pair perfectly vertical and footed with small plinth blocks; they were either left solid, hollowed out on the inner angle, or built up. When solid, they were often enriched with a low relief Chinese fret carved up the two outer faces—a treatment technically termed card-cut ornament (Fig. 78).

When the legs were hollowed out or built up, the outer faces were pierced with similar frets, and often appear extremely fragile. A turned shaft was in some cases set in the hollow leg, which in section was L shape, the shaft occupying the angle between the arms of the L. Fretcut brackets were usual in the angles between the legs and seat frame, the latter being sometimes faced with a strip of mahogany, card cut or pierced with frets.

* Chambers was subsequently knighted; he was also appointed Royal Architect, in which capacity he executed many important commissions, notably Somerset House, wherein the exhibitions of the Royal Academy were held for some years.

The stretchers were of the plain rectangular section, frequently fret cut.

According to the particular design, the trellis panels of the back and beneath the arms were either fret-sawn out of one board or were built up to some extent.

Among the many designs of the Chippendale school, particularly those of country origin, a favourite treatment of the back was to repeat the slightly undulating top rail in three or four rails at lower levels framed into the back uprights. This composed the ladder back. In the best examples the top and ladder rails were carved with narrow scrolls and leaf edging bordering slight piercings, the latter often being absent in the top rail.

In the plainer country types the carving was omitted and the piercings enlarged, if present at all.

Such chairs had square legs, often with a wave moulded surface on the two outer faces of the front pair, and four plain stretchers. The seat was stuffed over the rails or on a drop-in frame, and frequently was dipped (Fig. 79).

The moulding worked on the leg faces was often repeated on the back uprights and the arm supports, but it is not uncommon to find it present on the back members while the legs are plain but for a tiny ovolo worked on the outer arris (Figs. 76 and 81). This latter moulding is also found carved in rope and bead patterns, and, as with the wave moulded leg and uprights, appears on chairs with pierced and carved splats.

The ladder-back chairs in mahogany can generally be dated after 1760 (the type being also a favourite for many years in country specimens in oak, ash, walnut, and elm).

They must not be confused with a farmhouse and cottage rush-seated chair with ladder back, which was based on Dutch models and became very general in use among the labouring classes during the second half of the century. Such chairs are, nevertheless, quite beautiful things in

125

their quiet way, constructed in oak, elm, and ash to withstand any amount of hard wear.

To return to the fashions. Many chairs were made in which the French, the Gothic, and the Chinese tastes were mingled together. Some show a foretaste of the Adam manner also; the varieties from 1750 to 1770 being very numerous (Figs. 76, 77, and 81).

The upholstered chairs (*i.e.*, in addition to the stuffed seat) must next be considered.

The early specimens (*circa* 1725–1730) in walnut and in mahogany, exhibiting the lion mask on the knee of the leg and at the projecting arm end, continued the Queen Anne plain stuffed-over back (Fig. 73) with seat to match—generally covered in needlework or damask. The wood of the arms was on many entirely exposed, but a frequent practice was to stuff or pad the horizontal member, leaving the support exposed, which was carved in prevailing fashion. To suit the enormous dimensions of ladies' dresses, the arm support was swept rapidly backward as it rose to the arm, and this provided a field for fine carving (Fig. 78).

On other chairs the arm space was padded solid. The height of the back was now always lower than on those in fashion until *circa* 1730.

The dining chairs were designed with quite liberal seats, but the upholstered chairs were still more roomy, and the proportions were very different owing to the seat being lower as well as broader and deeper. Such chairs were made throughout the changing fashions of classic, French, Gothic, and Chinese tastes.

A very distinct type of chair was introduced about 1720 for writing purposes. The usual design had a square seat, two sides of which were open to the sitter, while the other two sides were enclosed by turned uprights rising from three of the legs. The tops of the uprights were connected by a horizontal built-up rail, semicircular on

126

FIG. 81.—AN ARMCHAIR IN MAHOGANY (*c.* 1770–75).

*A type of chair showing the transition from Chippendale to Hepple-
white fashions ; the back uprights curve over to a " camel-back" top
rail on which a central rosette with trailing husks are carved in low
relief.*

*The splat is still united to the seat by a shoe-piece ; its simple form
is suggestive of earlier work, but this vertical piercing was returning,
enriched with ribbon husk and other motifs. The seat frame is dipped
and holds a drop-in seat.*

The property of Stanley J. May, Esq.

FIG. 82.—A MAHOGANY CHAIR (*c.* 1775).

The back constructed in the heart shape, the curved members being sunk on face with a tiny bead worked on the edges. Very delicate carving is cleverly placed.

The front legs are panel sunk on the taper and finish on spade feet.

The seat is stuffed over, the covering being secured by two rows of brass-headed nails.

(*a*)   (*b*)

FIG. 83.—TWO MAHOGANY CHAIRS IN THE "HEPPLEWHITE" STYLE.

(*a*) *Is a specimen showing transitional features. The splat is connected to the seat and the legs to each other by stretchers; the legs, however, show the slight taper (c.* 1770).

(*b*) *Is a fully developed chair of the style c.* 1775. *The back is shield-shaped, connected only to the stumpy continuation of the rear legs; the legs taper and are devoid of stretchers.*

In both chairs the back members are face moulded. The splats are alike in character and the slight low-relief carving. The wheatear and husk drop on (b) is the more usual.

The property of Messrs. Wm. Morris & Co.

FIG. 84.—A PAINTED CHAIR (*c.* 1785-90).

The back composed as an oval wheel. The seat is stuffed over on a dipped and serpentine frame. The legs taper quickly, and in front are fitted with collar pieces in place of the spade foot.

The property of Edward Hudson, Esq.

plan, and about 12 inches above the seat; it had a flat top surface, and on the centre third of its length was thickened or covered with a shaped block, well rounded off to give comfortable support. The two ends of the top rail were finished either in a plain horizontal scroll or scrolled over and carved. The two spaces between the three uprights were filled with shaped, pierced, and carved splats rising from the normal shoe-pieces. The seat was upholstered on a drop-in frame (Fig. 80).

The legs were various in design and arrangement. Usually all four legs were plain square, with the tiny ovolo running up the outer arris, and with plain stretchers crossing at right angles, when contemporary with dining chairs similarly legged.

Fine examples had all four legs cabriole, variously carved; others had the one leg cabriole that comes under the front corner of the seat, while the remaining three legs were left plainly square or taper turned with pad feet, such being without stretchers as a rule.

Many writing chairs were made in walnut.

Soon after 1765 the refining influence of Robert Adam began to make itself felt among chair and cabinet makers. In many ways it was very salutary, for the rococo designs were becoming extremely fantastic, and much absurd work was at least contemplated, to judge by designs produced by Ince and Mayhew and others.

Between 1765 and 1770 Adam designed some excellent chairs in connection with the furnishing of mansions then being erected under his direction.

At first he was guided as to general shapes by Chippendale models, but he at once modified and refined the splat, some being of lyre shape. He employed but little carving elsewhere.

The shaped top rail of the preceding twenty years he used at first, but quickly replaced it by curved forms such as ovals, or a top of three loops, the central loop

127

crowning the splat, which still rose from a shoe in the seat rail.*

Adam was also partial to a chair back of square outline, the uprights and top rail being of square section and delicately moulded; here, again, a restrained splat occupied the space.

On his mahogany chairs he usually placed the square tapering leg, which, at the level of the seat rail, had an oval patera carved in a sunk panel or applied. A cavetto mould was cut on all faces of the leg immediately below the seat, and upon the uninterrupted taper simple flutes were cut which stopped just above a moulded plinth cut in the solid.

Seat rails were moulded when not stuffed entirely over; on some he repeated the Vitruvian scroll previously used by Kent; he also reintroduced caning for seats.

Adam chairs were often inlaid with delicate classical detail, or when made in beech were painted with similar motifs, honeysuckle and husk ornament being favourites.

For upholstered chairs Adam largely designed on French lines, with oval back frame of moulded wood stuffed in, and upholstered, together with the seat, in tapestry patterned with classical detail. The seat was oval or circular and stuffed over, yet showing a moulded lower frame running into square blocks at the tops of the legs. The oval back frame was held by tenons on the short moulded continuations of the turned rear legs. The front legs were also taper turned, but above the seat rail they rose in square section, serpentine curved, to support horizontal bowed arms which had a padded top. These arm supports and the legs were fluted, the latter terminating in small, swell-turned feet. The construction of such chairs was generally beech, and invariably they were entirely gilt.

* In the case of the oval back, the splat was contained within the oval and was entirely disconnected from the seat rail.

FIG. 85.—A MAHOGANY CHAIR (*c.* 1790) SHOWING THE
TRANSITION FROM "HEPPLEWHITE" TO "SHERATON"
DESIGNS.

*The latter style being more productive of rectangular back
shapes the than curved forms. The looped drapery and the
introduction of a low cross rail indicate the last decade of the
eighteenth century. The spade foot is retained in this case
but the taper is more severe.*

The property of Frank Partridge, Esq.

FIG. 86.—A PAINTED CHAIR (*c.* 1795).

The back is of typical rectangular form with lattice-bar work. The turned arm supports rise from the side rails and are too high to allow of S-*shaped arms. The front legs are turned and, like the arm supports, are also fluted. The seat is caned.*

FIG. 87.—A PAINTED CHAIR (*c.* 1795–1800).

*The front legs are delicately turned, with continuations forming
supports to the* **S**-*shaped arms.*

*The back uprights are parallel but sweep backward, terminating
in plain scrolls. The top rail is turned and shaped concave to the
back. The horizontal splat is an arrangement of bars, spindles,
and a decorated panel. The seat is caned for a squab cushion.*

FIG. 88.—A MAHOGANY CHAIR IN THE EMPIRE STYLE
(*c.* 1810).

The effect is produced by shaping members of rectangular section, mouldings being restricted to the turned and rope-twisted back rails. Brass ornament is applied on the flat back rail and in the form of rosettes at the sides of the uprights and the " knee " of the seat frame. A squab cushion is intended to cover the caning.

The property of R. Randall Phillips, E~q.

From about 1770 the designs of George Hepplewhite were contemporary. He realized the undoubted popularity of the fashions created by Robert Adam, and worked to supply the growing demand for elegant, light-looking chairs (Fig. 82).

The majority of his chair backs followed the constructive principle of the Adam oval back, inasmuch as they derived their support from the upward continuation of the back legs, and dispensed with a splat connected to the seat. Some examples, however, retained the earlier treatment (Fig. 83*a*).

His favourite back shapes were the shield, the oval, and the heart, with various open-work splats; every member being curved work necessitated the utmost care in selecting the wood and perfect construction. The faces were slightly sunk or moulded, and excellent carving in low relief was placed in well-considered positions, notably the husk, honeysuckle, wheat-ear, palmette, and other simple leaf forms (Figs. 81 and 83). The Prince of Wales's feathers were also present on chairs of this period.

In certain forms of chair backs, such as three interlaced ovals, the jointing and direction of the grain was obscured by a cross-banded veneer of mahogany on the front face.

Generally the legs tapered slightly and were of square section, often without the connecting stretchers. Fine taper legs were fluted or panel sunk, with plinth feet. Another type of Hepplewhite style leg was turned and fluted in the French-Adam manner; where these occur on armchairs the arm supports are invariably turned.

Seats continued to be stuffed over or on a drop-in frame, but the latter was rapidly going out of fashion *circa* 1775. The covering materials were now horsehair and mohair cloths, also silks, and when stuffed over the rails brass-headed nails were a usual edge fixing.

Whereas in the earlier mahogany chairs the arm supports invariably rose from and were screwed to the side rails of the seat, on many of Adam and Hepplewhite type they carry up from the front legs just an inch or two above the seat, when they suddenly sweep backwards and up to the shaped arm in a long concave curve; in other cases the arm support remained serpentine in shape.

Contemporary with Hepplewhite there were many excellent chair-makers, notably Shearer, Gillow, Mainwaring, and Seddon, Sons and Shackleton; all were producing similar work to that illustrated in Hepplewhite's book, and of superb quality.

The rectangular square-cornered back shape of Robert Adam was used by the Hepplewhite school with a row of vertical bars for a filling, but the finer chairs were now made with the top rail ramped at each side, the centre portion being a narrow horizontal panel. In such chairs the splat work was fairly restrained, being a set of narrow bars with formal loops of drapery or other features of classic origin, which rose from a low cross-rail a few inches above the seat (Fig. 85).

Many chairs were now being made for the drawing-room and bedrooms in beech, entirely covered with painted or lacquered ground, and ornamented with sprays, husk lines, pateræ shapes, etc., painted over or gilt.

The square-backed Hepplewhite chairs represent the later designs, and were fashionable about 1788. They are very similar to many mahogany chairs made after 1790, and it is often impossible to separate them.

Thomas Sheraton came to London in 1790. He had undoubtedly been trained as a cabinet-maker, but it seems doubtful whether, on coming to the Metropolis, he actually engaged in practical work. He was a keen student of the earlier eighteenth-century designs, a competent draughtsman, and possessed very definite ideas upon taste in furniture and decoration. His whole effort was toward light and graceful effects, relying upon perfect material and construction to make up for an almost dangerous reduction of mass. His designs, however, if somewhat effeminate in comparison with his predecessors', are full of character, and mark the last phase of inspired work in English furniture.

As with the Hepplewhite chairs, those of Sheraton design were produced in great variety. Generally, as regards the treatment of the back, he did not repeat the shield and heart shapes, but reproduced the rectangular forms, lightening them still further with various semi-classic splats or cross-rails, often inlaid and carved very delicately. Some top rails were turned—generally accompanied by uprights that scroll back at the top. A variation of the splat was a filling of trellis bars (Fig. 86); also between pairs of horizontal bars, rows of small balls or pierced circles were placed (Fig. 87). Another type had caned backs (when the seat was caned) either in oval or rectangular frames.

The arms did not join the back uprights squarely, but repeated some Hepplewhite patterns in being swept up to join the upright near its top. When the arm support was shaped as a concave curve rising above a square leg, the junction with the arm was angular, but the majority of Sheraton arms were of S shape (to side view), and rose from a daintily turned extension of a taper turned and moulded front leg (Fig. 87). These S arms, when viewed from above, are found to curve in serpentine form, which very cleverly obviated what would otherwise have been an awkward-looking joint with the back upright, owing to the front of the seat being wider than the back. About 1800 the S arms were reeded on the upper surface, this being repeated on the uprights.

On chairs of light construction the rear legs were also turned; on dining chairs they were rectangular and curved well backwards, but were quite devoid of the curves on the transverse plane so characteristic of chairs from *circa* 1740 to 1770 (omitting those in the Chinese taste).

MAHOGANY FURNITURE

It is important to notice the character of eighteenth-century turning. During the early mahogany and Chippendale periods, excepting the tripod stems, etc., it had practically no place in fashionable work, but Robert Adam, after his earliest designs, employed it increasingly throughout his extensive practice. It shows at once a quality of delicate refinement quite unknown in the crude turning of the oak period or in the masculine boldness of Wren and his followers. During the periods of Hepplewhite and Sheraton the turning became still more delicate, all curves being remarkably flat, fillets and astragals kept strictly to proportion, and often quite minute.

These qualities should always be looked for in the work of the 1770–1800 period, and when compared with the turning of 1820 and onwards the difference is so great as to suggest a lapse of a century instead of merely twenty years.

From *circa* 1800 the top rail of the chair back was often cut out of a rectangular strip about 4 inches wide, and rode over the back uprights, on to which it was fixed by tapering dovetails slotted into the back. This overriding of the back uprights is interesting, inasmuch as the late oak chairs and also those of late Carolean design followed precisely the same course.

This late Sheraton top rail was generally enriched with a sunk moulded border, a feature also applied to the lower cross-bars of the back.

Some fine chairs in the Sheraton styles were constructed in solid satinwood, which had already been employed for Adam and Hepplewhite designs. Frequently they were inlaid and painted, and as with painted beech chairs, the Sheraton feeling was more naturalistic than that favoured by Adam; they appear either in colours on a cream ground or *vice versa*, and in some instances the wood was lacquered and the sprays, figure subjects, etc., were in gilt.

Various leg stretchers were used, particularly on

132

painted chairs, many of them recalling the curved **X** forms of the William and Mary period. But the majority of late mahogany chairs were free of them.

The Sheraton types include the Empire phase, which came in about 1805, and is often termed Regency period. Sheraton himself made many designs in the Empire style; they are quite his worst efforts, and show him a slave to fashion, striving for novelty at all costs.

A favourite pattern with Empire chairs was to shape the front legs in bold concave curves, with a gradual taper and projecting forwards to balance the rearward curves of the back legs. At the sides the legs and seat frame were quite flush, the latter being dipped and forming one continuous curve with the knee of the front leg and the bow of the back upright without break in the line. The uprights usually scrolled over at the top, and were connected by flat or turned cross-members, the former often inlaid or faced with brass ornament, and the latter enriched with a spiral reeding or rope twist (Fig. 88).

Many turned cross-bars are concave to the back, but as the grain remains straight the ends must have been turned in separate operations, sufficient stuff having been allowed to shift the lathe centres. The centre part was twist turned, or moulded. Seats were generally caned and fitted with a squab cushion.

When arms were fitted, a general design was the Sheraton **S** shape, but instead of the turned support the arm curved down in a circular arc, which just touched the seat frame and continued to finish in a small scroll. This was weak construction, as it was impossible to avoid short cross-grain at the front curve of the arm, nor possible to obtain a thoroughly secure joint with the seat frame.

Other arms were straight with a scroll-over termination which was capped on a concave support, both being fluted or reeded; they were generally accompanied by legs which had squares faced with clumsy pateræ at the seat

133

frame, and were taper turned and reeded. In some cases seats and backs were upholstered, invariably in horsehair.

In addition to many chairs in mahogany or rosewood, they were still made in beech, painted and gilded.

Apart from the country-made chairs in oak, elm, ash, and beech, that were more or less reproductions of the fashionable types, there existed a quite distinct variety in which the rectangular mortice and tenon joinery did not play a part. I refer to the so-called Windsor chairs, and others with rush seats and backs with ladder slats or rows of spindles. The latter have been referred to on page 125 (Fig. 91 *a* and *b*).

Of the Windsor chairs, the early types had plainly turned stick legs or shaped cabriole, and the top bar of the back was shaped after the manner of mid-eighteenth-century mahogany chairs. Then followed the hoop back, and in the majority the filling was a set of upright circular rods on each side of a central fret-cut and pierced splat. This latter, when dating *circa* 1740–1760, is roughly Chippendale in feeling. Subsequent examples had a pierced circle or oval in the splat, usually filled with eight spokes like a wheel, or occasionally with a crude outline of the Prince of Wales's feathers. With these chairs the front legs were cabriole, or all were turned; they were connected with round stretchers, and from about 1750 that joining the front legs was often bent to a semicircle.

Those with arms had a horizontal bar of yew bent to a semicircle, through which all the back spokes or rods pass, the projecting side extremities being rounded off, and bent yew supports rake backwards from these ends down to the seat.

The frame of the hoop back was also of bent yew, and the splat was cut out of the same wood.

The back rods were generally beech, which was also used for legs and stretchers, though in some cases ash was used.

FIG. 89.—A WINDSOR ARMCHAIR
(c. 1775).

The seat is shaped out of one piece of
ash; it is bored with circular holes to
receive the socket ends of the turned legs
and the back supports. The carved
stretcher is of yew, bent to shape. The
legs are of beech, as also are the vertical
back rods. The hoop of the back, the
semicircular arm rail, and the cut and
pierced splat are of yew tree.

The legs should be compared with
Fig. 90.

FIG. 90.—A WINDSOR CHAIR
(c. 1790).

In this instance the Prince of Wales
feathers occupy the position in which a
wheel form is commonly found.

The ash seat (frequently it was of
elm) has a small projection at the back
which forms a seating for the two
raking strut rods passing behind the
vertical rods and stiffening the yew
hoop.

The turning of the legs and the
arrangement of stretchers conforms to
the ordinary type.

Victoria and Albert Museum.

(a) is an example of the ladder back, having six shaped rails diminishing in sizes as they descend. The front stretcher and the low arms are baluster turned. The front legs are circular with pad feet.

FIG. 91.—TWO RUSH-SEATED FARM-HOUSE CHAIRS BELONGING TO THE SECOND HALF OF THE EIGHTEENTH CENTURY: THEY ARE CONSTRUCTED OF ASH.

(b) is an example of the spindle back, arranged in two rows. The front stretcher is simply swell-turned, otherwise the framing is similar to (a). The club-footed legs are here raised on ball turning.

The property of William Harvey, Esq.

The seat was invariably a thick elm or ash board, dished out in familiar manner, and provided with a small projection at the back to take a couple of stick struts from the crown of the hoop (Figs. 89 and 90).

The framing of such chairs is known as stick construction, all joints being circular taper-fitting tenons in circular mortices. The ends were heated before being driven home, which ensured expansion on cooling and an extremely tight fit. On eighteenth-century Windsor chairs the leg tenons frequently came right through the seat, and showed as circles on the top surface.

The rush-seated chairs (Fig. 91) form another interesting type, though their construction is very similar to the Windsor chair.

Those with two sets of turned spindles between the tall back uprights are supposed to have emanated chiefly from Lancashire, the ladder-back variety being more general in the southern counties.

The early types from about 1725 to 1775 had legs turned with stout club feet in semi-cabriole form, but sufficient wood seldom was allowed to shape the knee.

These chairs were made in oak, elm, ash and occasionally in beech; and, like the Windsor chairs, were often left unpolished or unvarnished.

Windsor chairs were kept clean by scouring with sand, and this treatment applied generally to various types of kitchen chairs with wooden seats.

III.—SETTEES AND SOFAS

During the early Georgian period the settees were of two types, and, as they followed the chair designs, they varied but little from the late specimens of the walnut period; in fact, many settees continued to be made in walnut wood until *circa* 1730, or later.

The type with back composed of two or more chair backs continued to be popular throughout the eighteenth century, and specimens may be dated according to the resemblance they bear to the designs of contemporary chairs (Fig. 92).

The other type was the elongation or widening of the upholstered chair. The backs, until *circa* 1750, were stuffed over, and when high were generally straight. When the back was lower, the top line was serpentine or undulating, and was often swept in with the arms.

In many cases, especially those showing Kent influence, *circa* 1735–1740, the seat frame was exposed and carved; other rich specimens had the back stuffed within a shaped frame, which, together with the arms, seat frame, and legs, was richly carved and gilt, the covering material being damask.

The arms were either solid, stuffed, with scroll-over top, or had a pad on the horizontal member, which left the forward end and support exposed. From 1750 the rococo ornament, then at the zenith of popularity, was freely employed, together with less ornate carving, such as small acanthus, C scrolls, gadrooned seat edging, etc.

Many fine sofas—for that is their title in the trade catalogues after 1750—were very long, and frequently

136

FIG. 92.—A MAHOGANY SETTEE OF THE TWO-CHAIR-BACK TYPE (*c.* 1760).

The type of top rail and treatment of the splat indicate a late date.

The square legs (the central leg is tapered) have angle brackets in the Chinese taste.

The arms show a continuance of the forms adopted early in the century.

FIG. 93.—AN UPHOLSTERED COUCH (c. 1790).

The framing is veneered in satinwood with border bands of mahogany.
Turning is entirely absent ; the lines are severe but of delicate and refined proportions.

had four front legs. The shaped top rail of the back and the front face of the arms were left exposed and carved, to accord with the enrichment of the curved seat framing.

Beech was the usual wood used in building up the framework, mahogany being employed only for exposed parts when entire gilding was not intended.

The restraining influence of Adam was in evidence after 1760; the overwrought rococo rapidly gave way before simple lines, well considered in mass and proportion, with ornament of great delicacy applied as veneer, inlay, carving or painting.

This manner set the taste for the remainder of the century, and was adapted equally well to the chair-back types and those with upholstered backs and seats. Some were veneered in satinwood with mahogany or tulip cross-banded borders (Fig. 93).

Empire settees were designed similarly to the chairs, and, as in the earlier periods, were often made en suite with a set of chairs. There was also a return to the day-bed type, in which a low upholstered back was carried into a high roll-over end with the front face exposed in moulded and scrolled mahogany.

IV.—TABLES

DURING the eighteenth century new requirements for tables came into being, with the result that the number of varieties increased; but this was much more the case in the second than in the first half of the century.

DINING TABLES.—Of primary importance is the dining table. The Queen Anne fashion of using a number of small tables was declining during George I.'s reign, and, instead, a gradual reversion to the long extending table took place.

The gate leg played the most important part in their construction, but it was of a new sort. The old type of framed gate was still largely used in country districts, but the fashionable gate table from about 1720 was made in mahogany or walnut, having four or six cabriole legs, two or four being fixed to a narrow rectangular under frame, and on each of the long sides an extra leg swung out on an arm of the under frame, these two legs being tenoned above their knees to the arms, and pivoted by wooden hinges on the main frame (Fig. 94). The top was, therefore, similar in form to the older type gate-leg table, usually oval or circular, composed of a central fixed board and two flaps, with an ovolo or ogee moulded edge. The ancient method of dowel fixing the table top was by now superseded by the metal screw. On the sides of the under frame, at regular intervals, slanting grooves were gouged out which provided a starting-point for screws, which were driven in until they entered the thickness of the top and held it securely in place. Likewise in the mortice and tenon joints of the framing the dowel pins were generally omitted, and hot thin glue was applied to the members composing the joint immediately before assembling and cramping up.

138

FIG. 94.—A MAHOGANY DINING TABLE (*c.* 1730).

The top is circular when extended, the two flaps being supported on gate legs.

The six legs are of cabriole form, carved over the knees with acanthus and side nulling. The feet are claw and ball finely carved.

This type of table was also made with four legs.

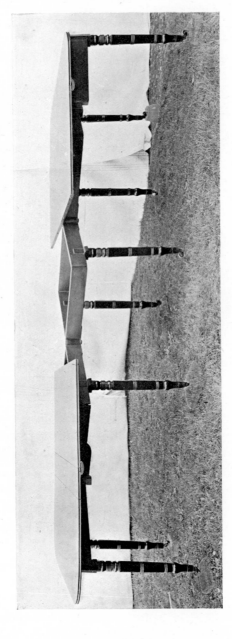

FIG. 95.—A MAHOGANY EXTENDING DINING TABLE (*c.* 1805).

The illustration shows the table fully extended—11 ft. long by 4 ft. 3 in. wide—and two of the four extra leaves are removed to show the lattice action underframing. It will be noticed that the four intermediate legs arrange themselves beyond the reach of the sitters' knees. By removing the four leaves the table will fold up to form an ordinary side table only 22 in. deep.

The property of Stanley J. May, Esq.

These changes in workshop practice affected all types of furniture, though dowelling the tenons lasted long in country districts, and is to be found in the seat rail joints of some mahogany chairs.

Reverting to the gate-leg dining table, simple specimens had circular taper legs with pad feet, after the model of many rear legs to early eighteenth-century chairs.

Soon after the introduction of square legs on chairs the plain square leg appeared on these tables; they were generally made of Cuba or San Domingo mahogany, each section of the top being out of one piece, and were very heavy and quite rigid.

Other tables, in order to increase the maximum length, were composed of three units, the centre unit being a double-gate table with rectangular flaps, on each side of which a semicircular pier-type table could be fitted having four fixed legs; this provided a long table with semicircular ends.

Dining tables for great establishments were built up on this unit principle, and necessitated a great number of legs.

Many mahogany dining tables *circa* 1770–1800 were of beautifully figured wood with inlaid and cross-banded borders.

Towards the close of the eighteenth century attempts were made to produce extending dining tables in which the leaves only were detachable, and some very ingenious devices were worked out. The majority were worked by a sliding under frame, and, being excellently made, ran pretty smoothly, although devoid of the central screw action of the modern table.

About 1800 some tables were designed with a clever lattice-shaped under framing, entailing the manufacture of special brass hinges. They were capable of holding four or five extra leaves, and at the other extreme of collapsing into an ordinary side table, the travel and final disposition of the eight legs being quite a geometrical problem (Fig. 95).

139

During the influence of Robert Adam, the usual leg was the taper with plinth or spade foot; occasionally they were turned, but this treatment was more frequent after 1800.

Generally speaking, contemporary dining tables and sideboards had something in common, being practically the only important furniture of the eighteenth-century dining-room, with a fine set of ten or a dozen mahogany chairs to complete the scheme.

Another type of dining table dates from about 1790, and was often made in pairs for large rooms. The top was oval or rectangular, reeded around the edge, and carried on bearers, which were hinged by means of pins to the rectangular block at the top of a stout turned column. The pins could be withdrawn and the top removed. The column was supported by four concave or serpentine legs reeded on the top surfaces; the extremities of the legs were capped with brass lion-claw castors.

SIDE TABLES.—The side table was an essential in the dining-room during the first half of the eighteenth century, for until *circa* 1755 the sideboard had not been designed as a distinctive piece of furniture.

Similar types were the console and pier tables, both the latter being placed against the piers or masses of solid wall between the tall sash windows. Over these tables a pier glass was hung, tall in shape, and generally in gilt frame. The side tables, therefore, whether for duty in meal service or as a pedestal for fine china, were considered important, and much excellent work was expended on them. Of the early mahogany period, some had richly carved cabriole legs, wholly or parcel gilt; but the majority had massive scroll-shape legs, placed either singly at the corners, grouped in threes, or solidly connected in truss forms. They owed much to Kent's influence, and bore the heavy architectural character already referred to.

In certain rare cases the entire stand was treated as a composition in sculpture.

FIG. 96.—A FINE MAHOGANY SIDE TABLE (*c.* 1750).

The frame is serpentine in front, with frieze veneered in mahogany and faced with the "pre-Chinese" fret. The bed mould is boldly carved with the egg and tongue on the ovolo, a feature retained from the earlier "architects'" furniture. The bead below the frieze is carved with the flower and ribbon. The legs are of graceful cabriole form, displaying an excellent example of the French cabochon and leaf on the knees. The shoulders are continued as a shaped apron finely carved with acanthus. The feet end in the whorl or French scroll. The top slab is of scagliola.

Frame: Width, 3 ft. Height, 2 ft. 7½ in. Depth, 1 ft. 7½ in.
Top, 3 ft. 2¼ in. × 1 ft. 10½ in.

The property of Percival D. Griffiths, Esq.

FIG. 97.—A SATINWOOD SIDE OR PIER TABLE OF SEMICIRCULAR FORM
(c. 1780–85) CLOSELY RESEMBLING THE DESIGN OF FIG. 101.

In this case the underframe is inlaid with a frieze of honeysuckle in geometrical repeats, the top being further enriched with the typical fan design. Circular rosettes are inlaid at the tops of the legs.

The tops were of marble; frequently it was of a manufactured sort termed Scagliola. Of this material Mr. Macquoid writes:*

" This manufacture was invented in Italy as a cheaper substitute for marble at the end of the sixteenth century, and was introduced here for furniture and decoration about 1735. It was a composition of calcined gypsum mixed with isinglass and Flanders glue; when in this state, it was coloured to imitate the different varieties of marble, and laid on like cement; after hardening, it was capable of a very high polish."

In England fragments of Derbyshire marble were frequently worked into the composition.

The sequence of design in side tables followed very much in the manner of the chairs. From about 1740 the lighter French and semi-classic detail was present on framing constructed less massively (Fig. 96). The cabriole leg was now more general, richly carved in conjunction with the frieze, on which the wave scroll is found as late as 1750. Gilding was still employed to cover the whole of the legs and framing when the construction was in soft wood.

Between 1750 and 1760 the marble top declined in favour (some of the latest examples have a drop-in marble slab on an Adam framework), and side tables, often of considerable size, were made entirely of mahogany for use in the dining-room.

Great refinement marks these tables during the Adam period: the top straight-fronted or serpentine, with frieze carved or fluted, the legs tapered and fluted, of square or round section, or faced with applied rosettes and husks.

In some cases a pair of corner tables, each upon three legs and with quadrant shape tops, were supplied en suite to round off the ends of the side table.

Semicircular topped side or pier tables were made in large numbers from *circa* 1770; they had four legs and were

* P. Macquoid, " The Age of Mahogany."

141

identical with contemporary card tables, except that the top was a fixture and all legs were immovable (Fig. 97). Shaped stretchers appeared on some of Adam design.

Turning to the varieties of small tables in mahogany, comparatively few appear to have been made in the early Georgian period. Tables veneered in walnut and with cabriole legs, described in Part II., were still retained in use. However, it was quite in the natural sequence that walnut shapes should appear in early mahogany; they can generally be recognized by the peculiar treatment of the frieze, which was shaped as a plain, hollow moulding with greatest projection at the top. Alterations in design appeared with the rising French influence from about 1735: the beautifully designed cabriole legs often carved on the knee with cabochon and leaf or with acanthus alone, the frieze enriched with card cutting, and the edge moulding of the top also carved about this time with the ribbon and flower. On others the shoulder blocks of the cabriole legs were connected along the bottom of the frieze with a gadroon carved moulding.

CENTRE TABLES.—Centre and side tables were often used for the display of china or for tea. From about 1750 a fret-cut gallery was affixed to the edges of the square or serpentine top. On some specimens this gallery formed the sides of a removable tray top.

Very frequently the whole design, more or less in Chinese taste, was carried out in fret cutting; the legs (now straight) had the two outer faces decorated with card cutting or were hollow, and pierced in geometrical designs, with or without a circular shaft contained within the angle rising from a solid plinth block (Fig. 98).

In the Gothic taste, legs were built up as a group of three circular shafts in two tiers, united by an intermediate block and square plinth. The frieze was also card cut or again pierced with intricate patterns, and X stretchers were provided and similarly cut. Fret-cut brackets were

FIG. 98.—A MAHOGANY TEA OR CHINA TABLE (*c.* 1760)
BELONGING TO THE CLASS KNOWN AS FRETTED
FURNITURE.

*With the exception of the top board all ʃarts are delicately fret cut,
and all sides are serpentine in shape.*

*The gallery, frieze, and cross stretchers are built up of veneer
laminations for necessary strength.*

Length, 3 ft.   Width, 1 ft. 11 in.

FIG. 99.—A MAHOGANY TRIPOD TABLE (*c.* 1760).

The top is solid sunk, with edge shaped and carved in "pie-crust" fashion. This is supported by a gallery on the central column upon which it can revolve in addition to swinging vertical.

The column and tripod feet are finely carved in prevailing fashion.

Diameter of top, 2 ft. 5 in.

Victoria and Albert Museum.

frequently fixed between legs and frieze. Usually the top only is of solid wood, and that may be veneered; the gallery, frieze, stretchers, and probably the pierced leg faces will be found composed of layers of mahogany veneer alternating in direction of the grain, so giving remarkable strength, exactly as in modern plywood.

About 1765 the fret-cut gallery disappeared, together with the pierced construction, and very soon afterwards the designs of Robert Adam appeared in simple tables with square or turned taper legs (the turned legs were often enriched with spiral fluting).

TRIPOD TABLES.—By the middle of the century the circular top tripod table was in great demand. Such a form was not new,* but was now receiving the attention of the skilled designers. The tripod foot in mahogany varied but little, having the appearance of three inclined cabriole legs, which were dovetailed into the base of the central column. The latter was turned in plain classic shape or of baluster outline, and the best examples were beautifully carved, not only on the stem, but also on the three legs, and the feet cut into claw and ball, lion's paw, and dolphin heads.

About 1755 an improvement was effected, whereby the top would not only revolve, in addition to being hinged, but by the withdrawal of a wedge could be lifted free of the tripod support. This was contrived by constructing a gallery which was hinged to the two cross-bearers on the under side of the top, and obtained a seating about the reduced apex of the central column and formed the bearing upon which the top could revolve (Fig. 99). This mechanism is set out in diagrammatic form on page 145, together with the various leg shapes and approximate dates.

* There is a tripod table at the Victoria and Albert Museum in pearwood with scroll legs belonging to the end of the seventeenth century.

143

For best work a fine single piece of mahogany was selected for the circular top, which was either sunk on the top surface, leaving a small raised mould at the edge, or, having been sunk, the edge was cut and moulded in small balancing curves, known as a " pie-crust " edge. Such would be used for tea, supper, etc.; others were for the display of china, and fitted with a fret-cut gallery.

Simple mahogany specimens, well turned on the stem, but entirely uncarved, were made continuously throughout the second half of the eighteenth century. Those made in oak and beech proclaim a remote country origin.

CARD TABLES.—I have already referred to the retention of the walnut type card table. The long cabriole legs provided an excellent field for beautiful carving over the knees, and up till about 1740 the lion mask was frequently employed for decoration (Fig. 100).

The pronounced rounded corners of the top, with supporting cylinders in the frieze, continued until about 1750. The square angle was introduced *circa* 1740, though still breaking out from the straight or serpentine sides. With the adoption of the square leg the top became rectangular or serpentine, with the moulded edge often carved. Those tables intended for dual use of card playing and tea had a couple of hinged flaps, the one felted and the other veneered. Some had a drawer.

The plain, taper-turned legs with pad feet are to be found on some early mahogany card and tea tables. When closed, the table was of semicircular form with two flaps, the first to swing over, and usually of solid mahogany; the second, also solid, was hinged on butts as a lid to the box formed within the under framing. Three legs were permanently fixed to the semicircular under frame—two on the straight " back " frame, and the third placed centrally on the curve; the fourth leg was mortised to a gate arm of the " back " frame, pivoted on a wooden hinge to swing out and support the flap (see diagrams, p. 180).

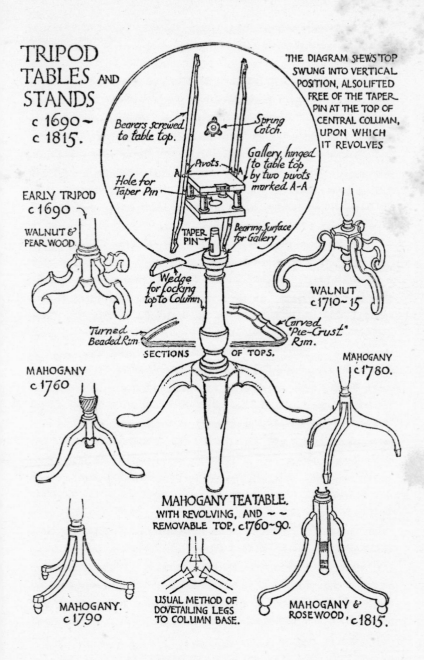

TRIPOD TABLES AND STANDS
c 1690 ~ c 1815.

THE DIAGRAM SHEWS TOP SWUNG INTO VERTICAL POSITION, ALSO LIFTED FREE OF THE TAPER PIN AT THE TOP OF CENTRAL COLUMN, UPON WHICH IT REVOLVES

Bearers screwed to table top.

Spring Catch.

Gallery hinged to table top by two pivots marked A-A

Pivots.

A—— ——A

Hole for Taper Pin

Bearing Surface for Gallery

TAPER PIN

EARLY TRIPOD c 1690

WALNUT & PEAR WOOD.

Wedge for locking top to Column.

WALNUT c 1710~15

Turned Beaded Rim

Carved "Pie-Crust" Rim.

SECTIONS OF TOPS.

MAHOGANY c 1760

MAHOGANY c 1780.

MAHOGANY TEA TABLE.
WITH REVOLVING, AND ~~ REMOVABLE TOP, c 1760~90.

MAHOGANY. c 1790

USUAL METHOD OF DOVETAILING LEGS TO COLUMN BASE.

MAHOGANY & ROSEWOOD, c 1815.

In rare cases there were three flaps, when the circular top could be either of polished wood or felted as desired for cards or tea.

Until about 1765–1770, with the exception of the type just described, the extending legs were operated by elbow-jointed under-framing, as first used on walnut period card tables, but with the general adoption of the circular top, the two rear legs were attached each to a single arm of the under frame, similarly to the method employed on dining-table gates.

Some card tables were made in satinwood inlaid, and from about 1775 painted also.

The fashionable shape for play was now circular; this necessitated semicircular framing of pine, veneered either with mahogany or satinwood; the legs were inlaid where crossing the frieze, at first with pateræ and later (from *circa* 1785) with flowers in an oval or rectangle. The satinwood frieze was painted. The arrises of the legs and the top were inlaid with lines of box or holly, and the top flap was often inlaid with a large fan pattern in which the light woods were shaded by scorching in hot sand.

From about 1795 the tops were again straight-sided, but with boldly rounded corners without projections. The late taper legs were fitted with brass collars or stops on the wood about 3 inches up from the base. The veneering was less refined in treatment; in many cases the mahogany and satinwood were almost in equal proportions.

PEMBROKE TABLES.—The convenience of the two-flap arrangement of the little old oak gate-leg tables led to a revival in the form of the Pembroke table.* These came in about 1765, and were made in mahogany and satinwood. Some of the earliest, in the Adam manner, had turned and fluted legs, with slight carving such as pateræ at the sides

* The old form of gate-leg table was also translated into mahogany, with legs and stretchers turned in simple refined mouldings.

FIG. 100.—A FINE MAHOGANY CARD TABLE (*c.* 1740) OF THE
LION MASK PERIOD.

*The top is of rectangular form with projecting circular corners slightly sunk for
candles, and a dishing on each side also. The covering is petit-point needlework.*

*The cabriole legs are finely carved with lion masks on the knee and foliage on
the shoulder pieces; the acanthus depends from the mask, which below the knee
changes into the semi-natural representation of the animal's leg and terminates in
the claw foot.*

Height, 2 ft. 3 in.   Length of side, 2 ft. 6 in.

FIG. 101.—A FLAP TABLE OF THE PEMBROKE TYPE
(*c.* 1780–85).

*The surfaces of oval top and frieze are veneered in satinwood
with mahogany borders, that of the top being further enriched
with the classic honeysuckle border in the Adam manner. The
legs are of solid satinwood with mahogany borders. The flaps
are supported by wooden brackets pivoted on self hinges.*

of the drawer in the under-framing. Legs then became square tapered with line inlay, and were again turned and moulded about 1785. The top was of thin wood, and rectangular or oval in shape, the central fixed part being much larger in proportion to the flaps than earlier three-section table tops, owing to the flaps gaining support by one or two brackets, usually in beech, arranged to swing outward on wooden hinges. The flaps were hung on a pair of metal hinges, and closed on a rule joint (Fig. 101).

Many Pembroke tables were fitted with two drawers, one above the other, at one end, lined in thin oak or mahogany, and running on bearer strips screwed to the side frames. At the opposite end it was usual to form dummy drawer fronts by fixing handles and inlaying border lines on the deep frieze.

A large number of various small tables were made contemporaneously with the Pembroke, usually with turned or taper legs and fitted with a drawer in the frieze. Occasionally the top was serpentine or bowed, and in some dating from *circa* 1770 the legs are of the delicate French cabriole form, as applied to many fine chairs of the time, with carving on the flattish knee, which was swept in with a swell-shaped under frame.

DRESSING TABLES.—The bedroom furniture was seldom of mahogany before 1735, the small four-legged table, or the knee-hole table with drawers, serving as a stand for the mirror.

Mahogany chests of drawers, often with knee recess, were used for the toilet, in which the top drawer was specially fitted, including a collapsible mirror and reading stand. During the last quarter of the eighteenth century many fine dressing tables were specially designed to appear more like a drawing-room commode or writing table; even the mirror dropped into a slide at the back of the top, operated by a spring. They were made in inlaid mahogany or satinwood and in painted pine, the decoration of the

147

latter being a light ground tint with borders, wreaths, ribbons, etc., in contrasting colours (Fig. 102). Apart from these fashionable pieces, the mahogany dressing chest remained in favour, and upon which stood the separate mirror of oval, shield, or rectangular form.

WRITING TABLES.—In the second half of the eighteenth century the pedestal writing table, as distinct from the bureau, was very popular among the wealthy. Many magnificent examples exist, designed principally by Robert Adam, which in certain cases can be traced to the Chippendale firm.

The general form was that of a rectangular table with central knee-hole, and tiers of drawers on each side. The decoration of the side panels and of the drawer fronts corresponded with contemporary work on chests of drawers, wardrobes, etc.

Robert Adam set a fashion for a light type of writing table upon taper legs, with shallow drawers in the frieze; the top was surrounded on three sides with an upper fitment of small drawers, leaving a central space for writing covered in leather.

The light writing table was largely made from 1770 to 1800 minus the top fitment.

FIG. 102.—A DRESSING TABLE (c. 1790).

Semicircular in form and designed with central knee hole and flanking doors to appear like a commode. The slot for sliding mirror can be discerned at the back of the centre section of the top. It is constructed chiefly of pine with surfaces painted and with borders, wreaths, and swags also worked by the brush in contrasting colours.

FIG. 103.—A DUMB WAITER IN MAHOGANY (*c.* 1755).

The design of the lower part is exactly similar to many tripod tables. The two additional trays with their supporting columns are separate units. All three will revolve and they can be removed together with the two upper columns, their connections being a central dowel at the base of each shaft.

The trays were sunk on the lathe, leaving a small raised beaded edging.

> Diameter of top tray, 1 ft. 3 in.
> ,, ,, middle tray, 1 ft. 6 in.
> ,, ,, bottom tray, 2 ft.
> Total height, 3 ft. 6 in.

The property of Messrs. Wm. Morris & Co.

V.—SIDEBOARDS

THE sideboard proper, as distinct from the dining-room side table, was a product of the second half of the eighteenth century, though it had been forestalled by the oak dresser for very many years in the smaller country houses and farms. The side table still remained as an adjunct to the sideboard, but the marble top was being replaced by a solid board of San Domingo or Cuban wood.

The evolution of the sideboard from *circa* 1760 to 1805 is very interesting; on page 151 I have given a set of diagrams explanatory of the gradual change in form and arrangement. They may be outlined as follows:

1. The first idea was a retention of the side table, with the addition of flanking *detached* pedestals supporting urns of mahogany, lined with lead and fitted with drain-cocks (Fig. 104).

2. About 1765 the flanking pedestals became connected to the board. The urns were beginning to be fitted with numerous slots for knives, forks, and spoons, and owing to the practical difficulty of hinging a circular lid, a central tube was provided, with an inner lining to which the lid was secured, and by which it could be raised to get at the contents. Later, the shape became octagonal. Drawers began to be fitted in the frieze and also in the pedestals in lieu of the cupboard in some instances.

3. About 1770 the pedestals began to be modified, the supports being turned or taper legs arranged in threes or fours at each end—two in front, and one or two at the back. The leg designs followed contemporary chairs and tables, and gradually became shorter as the body became

149

higher in proportion. A lower drawer or cupboard was often fitted between the end pair of legs, the central bay being usually open below the frieze drawer to allow space for the standing wine cooler.

From 1770 the front was generally shaped, the favourite lines being a flattish bow, serpentine, and concave centre with convex flanking curves, or *vice versa*. This necessitated the shaping of cupboard and drawer fronts to agree with the curves of the framing, and entailed extra labour and care in cutting the dovetails. Drawers were lined with fine quality, thin, figured oak or Honduras mahogany.

Small sideboards were designed without a definite frieze; they had a centre shallow drawer with a single square cupboard or deep drawer at each side. These small specimens seldom can be dated prior to 1780 (Fig. 105).

The space beneath the central drawer was usually, though not always, arched at the corners by inlaid brackets, and when not entirely open was fitted with a shelf, which occasionally was enclosed with a tambour front after 1785.

A usual fitment to all these types, at the back of the top, was a brass rail raised about 12 inches on turned brass supports.

The decoration of the early sideboards was very restrained: the frieze was fluted and carved, and the pedestal cupboards were veneered and inlaid with border lines, ovals, etc.

About 1765 the pedestals became more elaborately inlaid, incorporating satinwood; cross-banded tulipwood was a frequent border; sycamore was largely used, and chestnut often as a substitute for satinwood. The shell inlay became popular during the last twenty years of the century.

Mr. Macquoid remarks* that it is unusual to find sideboards entirely of satinwood before the time of Sheraton (*i.e.*, from 1790).

* P. Macquoid, " The Age of Satinwood."

150

FIG. 104.—EARLY TYPE MAHOGANY SIDEBOARD (c. 1775).

Early type mahogany sideboard, consisting of long table upon six fluted taper legs, with detached flanking pedestal cupboards supporting urns. The urns are lined with lead and fitted with taps. The board is fitted with brass standards and rail for a curtain.

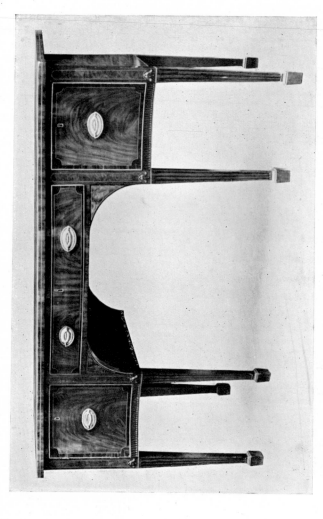

FIG. 105.—A SERPENTINE-FRONTED SIDEBOARD (c. 1780).

The body is constructed of pine, veneered in figured mahogany, with cross-banded borders, and inlaid with satinwood. The legs fluted in mahogany and tapered to spade feet. The accommodation consists of a wide central drawer, with deep drawer on right and cupboard on the left. The brass handles have stamped, oval, back plates.

Width, 5 ft.   Height, 3 ft. 2 in.   Depth, 2 ft. 6 in.

Victoria and Albert Museum.

FIG. 106.—A MAHOGANY INLAID SIDEBOARD (c. 1795–1800).

The four front legs appear to stand free ; they are turned and reeded in typical form.

The centre bay is recessed with concave corners, and is fitted with a long shallow drawer over the arch space intended for the wine cooler. The flanking drawers are set on convex curves, the whole five being inlaid with borders of satinwood.

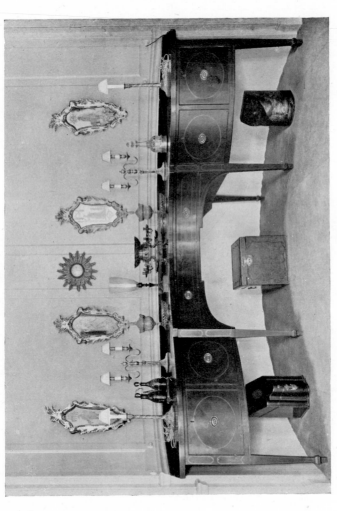

FIG. 107.—A MAHOGANY SIDEBOARD DESIGNED TO FIT A SEMICIRCULAR RECESS
IN THE DINING-ROOM (c. 1785).

*The surfaces are veneered and inlaid. The construction is in pine excepting the drawers, the fronts
of which are in mahogany, built up in the case of the flanking deep drawers and cupboards. The
mahogany legs are inlaid on the solid.*

Width (or diameter), 9 ft. 6 in.   Extreme depth (or radius), 4 ft. 8 in.   Depth of top in centre, 2 ft. 8 in.

The property of Edward Hudson, Esq.

DEVELOPMENT OF THE SIDEBOARD c1760~c1805.

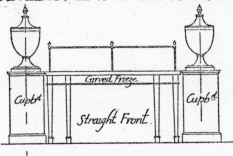

TYPE Nº 1

SIDE TABLE, FLANKED
WITH SEPARATE PEDES-
TALS WITH URNS.

c 1760.

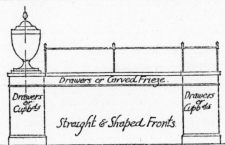

TYPE Nº 2

DESIGNED AS A COMPLETE
UNIT, WITH AND WITH-
OUT URNS AND RAIL.

c1765.

TYPE Nº3.

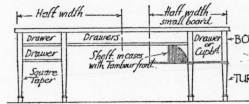

BOW AND SHAPED FRONTS.

c1770 ~ 1805.

TURNED LEGS AFTER c 1795

TYPE Nº 4

RETURN TO EARLIER
PEDESTAL TYPE, BUT
HEAVIER IN DESIGN

c 1805.

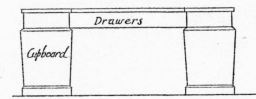

151

The edges of the top were usually square, cross-banded on the vertical, and with arris lines of contrasting woods.

Robert Adam, in designing his country and town mansions, was very partial to a large semi circular recess at the ends of rooms, and frequently planned such a space in the dining-room to receive the sideboard. It was, therefore, necessary in such cases to design this piece of furniture to fit the curve. Variety and interest were obtained by treating the front with convex and concave curves, producing a beautiful gradation of tone on the finely figured panels (Fig. 107).

With the exception of the legs, the carcase construction was in thoroughly seasoned deal or pine, and the drawer fronts of mahogany, often built up, upon which the veneers and inlays were glued down, the use of the hot caul being indispensable in such work; borders were frequently cross-banded and joined on the mitre. Drawer pulls were in brass, on a moulded and chased rose, prior to 1778, after which the back plate was of stamped brass, in all cases of formal design, based on the classic ideals of Robert Adam. The keyholes were faced with the thread escutcheon.

With the Empire period sideboards returned to the solid pedestal type and became very massive; the proportions seem ill-considered, and the ornament rapidly declined in quality. Though still very well constructed, they went from bad to worse, culminating in Victorian abominations, upon which, unfortunately, the finest Cuba wood was all too freely used.

VI.—CHESTS OF DRAWERS: SINGLE AND DOUBLE

CHESTS of drawers, as approved by the patrons of Queen Anne walnut, were not possible of much variation in regard to construction; they still remained of plain rectangular form when made in solid mahogany from about 1730.

The most important change lay in the abandonment of the low, table-like stand.

The early mahogany chests usually contained four or five drawers of the full width, and stood upon bracket feet, or occasionally upon stumpy cabriole legs.

A type of tall and narrow chest was made which might be termed a " tallboy," but, unlike the usual type, the carcase was in one piece.

In the second half of the century the chests were often taller and with five or six drawers, two of them being of half width placed at the top.

Their construction was perfect; the carcase was usually of pine, veneered, and framed by continuous dovetailing along all four angles of sides with bottom and top. The divisions between the drawers were solid from front to back, framed into grooves in the sides, and faced with mahogany strip or veneer.

The drawer linings were constructed in fine quality English oak, quarter sawn, and beautifully dovetailed (see diagrams, p. 177). On some late eighteenth-century examples the linings were of mahogany or of pine. When the chest was flat-fronted, the drawer fronts were either of solid mahogany, or curl mahogany veneered on plain

153

Honduras, oak, or pine; but when the front was bow or serpentine, the drawer fronts were veneered on mahogany or pine shapes (usually the latter). A plinth mould projected at the base, and a smaller moulding surrounded the top edge, both of which, in fine examples, were carved.

The bottoms of small and narrow drawers throughout the period were in one piece, with grain running from front to back, and housed in grooves cut in the sides about ¼ inch above the bottom edge; this arrangement also applied to the large, full-width drawers (the bottom, of two or three sections glued together) up to a very late date in the century. But a new method had been introduced about 1775, the bottom being divided into two panels by a central bearer running from front to back, and grooved on each side to take the panel edges, the treatment at the sides being identical with the older method; the panels were thin and generally arranged with the grain running transversely. This method ensured the drawer, when full, would bear only on the side runners, and obviated sag in the middle. The backs of carcases were often panelled, at first in oak, and later in pine, but the majority found to-day have the back enclosed by old boarding nailed into the rebated sides and top.

A minor but important difference from the "walnut" practice was the provision of a face strip above the top drawers and below the bottom drawer, by which means all drawers appeared surrounded and separated by a narrow facing of the carcase.

The projecting lip mould of walnut type is found around many early mahogany drawer edges, but is invariably part of the actual solid front, and consequently is worked across the grain at the ends; the applied projecting cock bead was contemporary, and after 1745 was used almost exclusively, and remained for the rest of the century.

The classic, French, Gothic, and Chinese tastes found expression on chests of drawers, though usually restrained,

FIG. 108.—A SERPENTINE-FRONTED CHEST OF DRAWERS (c. 1760).

The drawers are of oak with shaped fronts cut out of mahogany, upon which are laid veneers of figured mahogany with cross-banded borders of kingwood (not apparent in the photograph). The top drawer is excellently fitted for purposes of the toilet. The canted corners are faced with a fret-cut enrichment carved with tracery, etc., in the Gothic taste. This feature taken singly places the date 1745–50, but this period is too early for the fine figure of the veneer and the cross-banded kingwood.

Width, 4 ft. 4½ in.   Height, 2 ft. 11 in.   Depth, 2 ft]   [The property of Percival D. Griffiths, Esq.

FIG. 109.—A MAHOGANY CHEST OF DRAWERS DESIGNED IN THE
STYLE OF A FRENCH COMMODE (c. 1760).

*The shape is serpentine both on front and sides, the three drawers also
conforming to this outline, with a slight central swell in addition. The face
of the lowest drawer is carried below the bottom boards, shaped and carved
in the French rococo manner. The supports are moulded and carved as
attenuated cabriole legs with scroll feet. The cast-brass handles are also in
the French style.*

FIG. 110.—A MAHOGANY CHEST OF DRAWERS (*c.* 1780).

The top drawer is designed in escritoire manner, i.e. *with fall front, the interior being fitted with small drawers, etc.*

The drawers are edged with cock beading and are oak lined. The oval mahogany mirror is of about the same date. It is supported on a serpentine box stand fitted with three drawers.

Chest : 2 ft. 9 in. wide ; 3 ft. 5 in. high ; 1 ft. 8 in. deep.

The property of Messrs. Wm. Morris & Co.

FIG. III.—EXAMPLES OF LATE SHERATON MAHOGANY
BEDROOM FURNITURE.

The chest has sides of solid mahogany ; the top and divisions of the front, together with the bowed drawer fronts, are of pine veneered in richly figured mahogany curl. The drawers are cock-beaded and lined with pine. The deep frieze above the top drawers and the reeded angles together with the ring handles swinging from the centres of stamped roses indicate an early nineteenth-century date.

Width, 3 ft. 6 in.   Height, 3 ft. 7 in.   Depth, 1 ft. 9 in.

The property of D. G. Rogers, Esq.

The cheval mirror has supports and stretcher very delicately turned and supported on shaped trestle feet. The frame is of deal faced with cross-banded mahogany of convex section.

Width, 2 ft.   Height, 1 ft. 9 in.]   [The property of the Author.

as the drawer fronts were left plain save for the handles, often finely wrought in brass, the enrichment being worked on the top and plinth moulds, and on the bracket feet, which in cases were cabriole in profile.

The divisions between the drawers were also faced with carved mouldings, and on fine chests of serpentine shape the corners were treated as narrow pilasters arranged across the angle and covered with applied carving or frets (Fig. 108).

The chest of drawers intended for use in reception rooms followed the French commode, and was similarly named. Chippendale bestowed great attention upon this class of furniture, and many of the period are identical in form with contemporary French specimens.

They were serpentine on front and sides, often with swelled contour on the drawer faces or the pair of doors which in some cases enclosed the drawers; the front corners were framed with long cabriole shaped posts, carved in the French manner, and with scroll foot, the bottom outline being also shaped and carved in rococo ornament (Fig. 109). The handles fitted to these pieces were quite un-English, though made in this country (chiefly at Birmingham), the brass founders and finishers also contracting for the French market.

Plain mahogany chests of drawers continued to be made throughout the second half of the century and into the nineteenth, both veneered and in solid mahogany; the bracket foot and plinth was retained, but about 1770 a French method was adopted, by which the plinth was omitted and the vertical corners carried down to the floor with a delicate outward curve at the base; with such the bottom line of the framing is invariably shaped (Figs. 110 and 111). Simple inlay, as applied to contemporary sideboards and tables, is to be found on the chests. From the first quarter of the century a writing slide had been fitted to many low chests, framed in oak or mahogany, and provided with tiny brass drop loops to pull out above the top drawer

(Fig. 112); about 1765 this was discontinued, and the top-drawer front was hinged at the bottom edge, which, by means of a brass quadrant working in a guide at each side, could be swung out to a horizontal position to serve as a writing flap. The whole drawer also pulled forward slightly, the interior being fitted with pigeon-holes and small drawers, etc., as in the slant-top bureaux. These escritoire drawers were very generally fitted to chests surmounted by a bookcase (Figs. 110 and 115).

During the satinwood period, *circa* 1770–1800, many fine chests were veneered in this yellow wood, decorated with inlays and with floral paintings.

The brass drawer pulls gradually changed in character in accordance with the prevailing styles; illustrations of the more usual types appear in Fig. 129.

It is interesting to note that the fashion of the walnut period of using key escutcheons of the same shapes as the back plates to the handles had ceased about 1730, after which date the keyhole was usually edged by a brass rim driven in flush, and known as a thread escutcheon; these were used throughout the remainder of the century, but when the ornate French handles were employed, chased escutcheons frequently accompanied them, and again, in the late stamped brass fittings, little oval or polygonal escutcheons were often fixed to rhyme with the shapes of the back plates which were then again in favour.

Late Sheraton chests were in cases very tall, sometimes with reeded quarter columns let in on the front corners; there was also a square cross-banded edge to the top, and an unusually wide frieze above the two top drawers. These late chests were bow-fronted or flat, often veneered with fine curl mahogany (Fig. 111). Frequently the bracket feet were substituted by turned feet; generally such may be dated subsequent to 1800.

The double chest or tallboy reproduced the late walnut designs with practically no alteration of form. The angles

FIG. 112.—MAHOGANY DOUBLE CHEST OR TALLBOY (*c.* 1745).

The cornice is of typical architectural type with dentil course.
The frieze has an applied fret-cut band, and the canted corners are
fluted.   The lower portion has a mahogany writing slide.   The
drawers are oak lined, the fronts being of pine faced with $\frac{1}{4}$ in.
thick mahogany, lip-moulded on the edges.

Height, 5 ft. $9\frac{1}{2}$ in.   Width, lower part, 3 ft. $5\frac{1}{2}$ in.

The property of Edward Hudson, Esq.

FIG. 113.—A MAHOGANY SECRETAIRE (c. 1785-90).

This design is that of a side table upon taper legs, with two drawers in the underframing, upon which is mounted a secretaire or bureau having a sliding cylinder cover and a writing slide which pulls forward. The interior is simply fitted without a central feature. The surfaces are veneered in mahogany with bandings of cross-grain tulipwood. The handles of the slide and cover are stamped brass knobs, while the drop loops to the drawers are cast metal and show the Adam influence.

Height, 3 ft. 4 in.　Width, 2 ft. 6 in.　Depth, 1 ft. 11 in.

Victoria and Albert Museum.

were often splayed, with applied frets, or fluted, with the grain *vertical*, and the cornice with large cavetto remained until *circa* 1735 (run *with* the grain). Many drawer fronts were still edged with the lip mould until *circa* 1745 (Figs. 112 and 114), after which date the cock bead became fully established.

In the second half of the century the double chest was not quite so fashionable, as the wardrobe with hanging accommodation was now in use, and in the large houses soon became exclusively the piece for keeping clothes; the tallboy, however, continued to be made in early form until the end of the eighteenth century.

Distinctions appeared in the cornice treatment shortly before 1750, the flat frieze being decorated with an applied fret; following this, the frieze was often cut with vertical flutes, and from *circa* 1780 was inlaid with the shell in oval reserves, and the corner splays were also inlaid. The handles, when original, are also a useful guide to the date; but, unfortunately, a very great number of the eighteenth-century chests of drawers were " improved " during Victoria's reign by taking off the old brasses, stopping the holes, and screwing on a plain turned mahogany knob.

VII.—BUREAUX

THE walnut bureaux with slant flap over a chest of drawers, which became very popular during the reigns of Queen Anne and George I., set a lasting fashion upon which mahogany bureaux were made throughout the rest of the eighteenth century.

The treatment of drawer fronts, plinth, and feet followed the variations of those members upon the chests of drawers, the cabriole shaped bracket foot being in fashion between 1740 and 1755. The bureau interior was variously fitted with small drawers, pigeon-holes, and a central cupboard with flanking pilasters, which together formed a movable unit released by a hidden spring, to disclose narrow pockets behind the pilasters. The sides were usually veneered in one piece; the flap had a veneer of picked curl figure, and retained the lip moulded edge; the bracket feet were invariably cut from solid mahogany (Fig. 114).

Comparatively few bureaux of this type were made or faced with satinwood, and consequently are very rare; they were first introduced about 1770 inlaid with classic ornament, which about 1780 gave way to painting on drawer fronts and the flap.

Mahogany bureaux dating from 1780 to *circa* 1800 retain the old form, sometimes with the bracket feet connected by a serpentine curve under the plinth mould. The drawer fronts and the flap were inlaid with borders, and often with an oval and shell in the centre of the latter.

Among the designs in the Sheraton style, in mahogany or satinwood, with inlaid decoration, was the substitution of a sliding cylindrical cover instead of the hinged slanting

158

This piece is constructed in the hard-grained Spanish mahogany with very little figure.

The cornice is enriched with the dentil course, and is surmounted by an angular broken pediment with wide central space about the pedestal. The doors are of oak, flush panelled and veneered with mahogany upon which the astragal mouldings, with concave corners, are planted. The bureau is well and simply fitted with small drawers and pigeon-holes. The central cupboard with side pilasters is built as a complete unit which pulls forward by releasing a spring in the cupboard, disclosing secret pockets behind the pilasters.

The drawers are worked with the lip mould on the solid around the fronts, and are oak lined.

The bracket feet are of cabriole profile.

Height, 7 ft. 2 in.
Width, 3 ft. 2 in.
Depth of bureau, 1 ft. 9 in.

The property of Messrs. Wm. Morris & Co.

FIG. 114.—A MAHOGANY BUREAU CABINET
(c. 1745).

The design of the glazing, with thin astragal bars, should be compared with Fig. 61.

The cornice is straight, with dentil course, and the cavetto bed mould cut into a series of pointed arches, commonly called the pear-drop cornice. The doors are veneered in cross-banded mahogany with tulipwood border. The back is panelled in pine.

The top drawer (appearing as two) is the fall-down front of an escritoire, the interior being excellently fitted. All drawers are veneered in mahogany of fine figure, with cross-banded borders of tulipwood and boxwood lines.

Total height, 7 ft. 6 in.
Width of chest, 3 ft. 9 in.
Height of chest, 3 ft. 8 in.
Depth of chest, 1 ft. 10 in.
Depth of bookcase,
1 ft. 2½ in.

The property of
Stanley J. May, Esq.

FIG. 115.—A MAHOGANY BOOKCASE UPON
A CHEST OF DRAWERS (c. 1785).

flap; this was introduced between 1785 and 1790, some specimens being made with a shallow drawer under the writing compartment and carried on slender taper legs (Fig. 113). The sliding cover was a quarter cylinder, constructed of segments of pine or mahogany glued up to form the curve and veneered; this operated on being lifted by knobs at the bottom edge, and travelled upwards and inwards on side tracks to occupy a position behind the pigeon-holes.

In some cases the cover was composed on the tambour principle—*i.e.*, a series of mahogany slats, rounded on face, and glued side by side to a backing of stout coarse linen or fine canvas.

VIII.—CABINETS

1. Upon Bureaux and Chests of Drawers.—The mahogany bureau cabinet repeated the late designs in walnut, but there was an early cessation of fitting mirrors to the cabinet door panels, which after 1730–1740 were either panelled in mahogany or clear glazed. Cabinets in the Kent architectural style had classic pilasters with carved caps and moulded bases fitted to the door stiles; the cornice and pediment were also elaborate and somewhat heavy. This treatment became lighter with the advance of French taste, *circa* 1740, and from this date until *circa* 1750 the panels were framed with a wavy inner edge on the stiles and rails, or the panel was framed in flush, veneered over the whole surface, and a panel effect obtained by planting on a narrow mould of wavy contour with applied carved acanthus sprays at the four angles. This latter arrangement continued until *circa* 1760.

The cornice, though still classic, was proportioned on a smaller scale, and the dentil course was generally present. On fine specimens a fret-cut and pierced cresting board was fixed, but this was discarded soon after 1750 and the broken pediment again became universal, the form of the pediment being angular, circular, curved, or swan-neck (Figs. 114 and 116).

The cabinet interiors were excellently fitted with pigeon-holes, shelves with divisions for ledgers, and small drawers.

From about 1765 the fashion changed in regard to the lower bureau section with oblique flap. Henceforth it was generally designed as a flat chest of drawers, the

160

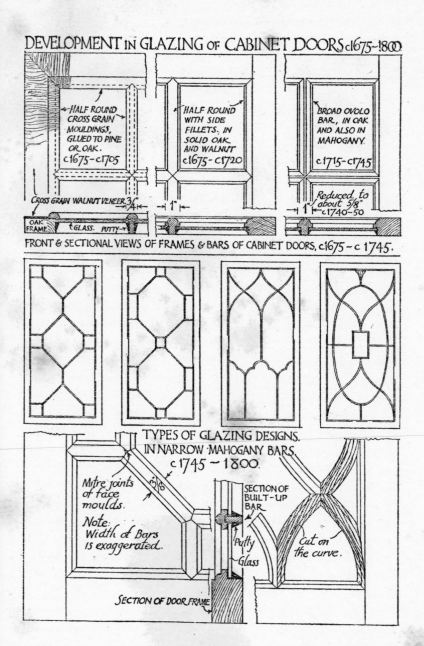

HALF ROUND CROSS GRAIN MOULDINGS, GLUED TO PINE OR OAK. c1675-c1705

HALF ROUND WITH SIDE FILLETS, IN SOLID OAK AND WALNUT c1675-c1720

BROAD OVOLO BAR, IN OAK AND ALSO IN MAHOGANY. c1715-c1745

Reduced to about 5/8" c1740-50

CROSS GRAIN WALNUT VENEER 3/4" — 1"

OAK FRAME t GLASS. PUTTY

FRONT & SECTIONAL VIEWS OF FRAMES & BARS OF CABINET DOORS, c1675 ~ c1745.

TYPES OF GLAZING DESIGNS. IN NARROW MAHOGANY BARS. c1745 ~ 1800.

Mitre joints of face moulds.

Note: Width of Bars is exaggerated.

5/8"

SECTION OF BUILT-UP BAR

Putty Glass

Cut on the curve.

SECTION OF DOOR FRAME

top drawer being deep, and hinged to swing out and pull forward as a writing flap (see note on chests of drawers, p. 156). The cylinder-top bureau also appeared, designed with a cabinet above, about 1790.

Cabinets fitted with a number of adjustable shelves for books and with glazed doors became very popular about the middle of the century, the doors, with some early exceptions, being divided by bars into panes.

From about 1750 the familiar thin mahogany glazing bars came in, coupled with a variety of shapes for the panes; the bars were usually of astragal section, not more than $\frac{3}{8}$ inch wide, and composed of two parts. A few of the bar designs will be found on the preceding page, where the evolution and arrangement of the glazing bar throughout the eighteenth century are set forth.

From about 1770 the door frames were often veneered with cross-banding and border lines of contrasting woods; also, from about this date, the lower or bed mould of the cornice was a cavetto cut into a series of pointed arches which spring from small turned half pendants glued on the frieze (Fig. 115). The backs of cabinets were generally panelled, at first with oak, and then in mahogany or pine.

The construction of the cornices of cabinets, wardrobes, tallboys, etc., of the mahogany period calls for special notice. They were all more or less classic in profile, and being run by hand with small moulding planes, were of necessity worked in separate units or tiers, and built up in position one above the other. This, in modern work, is rarely done, for with powerful moulding machines it is possible to cut the complete profile at one operation from a single board, which, when erected in a slanting position, gives the same effect.

2. DISPLAY CABINETS.—The mahogany glazed front cabinets for china, silver, etc., possess similar characteristics of form and construction to those supported upon bureaux and chests of drawers; but the lower part was

FIG. 116.—A MAHOGANY BREAK FRONT CHINA CABINET (*c.* 1795).

The side compartments of the cabinet are flat, while the centre is concave. The glazed doors have ornamental bar work in which loops of drapery and the Prince of Wales feathers are chief features.

The simple cornice has balustrading with urns on pedestals, and in the centre is raised to a swan-neck broken pediment, which contrary to tradition springs from the balustrade top mould. The frieze is fluted, with carved rosettes over the pilasters. The supporting cupboards, with drawers over, also have a concave centre, but the wings are convex, and beneath each pilaster a turned and carved column stands free and carries down to turned supports. Inlaid borders frame the doors and drawers. In addition the lower panels are inlaid with designs—ovals, vases, leaf scrolls, etc.

FIG. 117.—A MAHOGANY WARDROBE (*c.* 1765).

A simple specimen of the type designed with sliding shelves in the upper section over a chest of drawers.

The doors have flush veneered panels, bordered by an applied astragal moulding. The cornice is of typical section with dentil course. The drawers are lined oak. The base is the usual plinth mould and bracket feet.

Height, 6 ft. 2 in.   Width, 4 ft.

The property of Stanley J. May, Esq.

treated either as a range of drawers and cupboards with panelled doors supported on a plinth, or as an open stand framed with cabriole or square legs, varying in design with contemporary tables.

The cabinet doors prior to 1750 invariably had the heavy ovolo moulded glazing bars. The curved panel framing of 1740–1750 was also applied to glazed doors, with cross-bars of shaped outline.

Large china cabinets of the second half of the century were frequently designed with a break front (*i.e.*, a centre section projecting slightly in front of two separate wing units, and made separately in many cases) ; also various shaping of the fronts (involving bent glass in the doors), following the idea of the curves on contemporary sideboards (Fig. 116). Such were often beautifully inlaid on the frieze and the lower panels. They were also in satinwood inlaid and painted. In some instances the central top drawer of the lower section was fitted as an escritoire in the manner already described.

Another feature from *circa* 1785 was the attachment of turned and carved columns arranged in front of the pilaster strips which divided the doors and drawers of the lower part. In such cases the plinth was usually omitted, and the columns were carried down as turned feet (Fig. 116).

IX.—WARDROBES

EARLY mahogany wardrobes are scarce. A very limited number were made during the first half of the eighteenth century, largely owing to the retention of walnut furniture in the bedrooms, which often included a cupboard in addition to a tallboy. As already mentioned, the latter continued in mahogany for many years, but was augmented in its use as a clothes press by cupboards fitted with sliding shelves mounted upon a chest of drawers.

A few early specimens of hanging wardrobes were made with doors the full height, but these were not general until the last quarter of the century.

Many wardrobes dating *circa* 1740–1760 had the panels flush with the framing, often finely veneered and bordered with applied wavy mouldings with gaps at the corners, where leaf carving was applied. The cornice was frequently surmounted by a fret-cut cresting.

Large wardrobes from *circa* 1750 were constructed with a break front in three sections, the centre part being formed as a clothes press on a chest of drawers, the wings being arranged as hanging cupboards, with long doors.

Also from about this date the cornice was pedimented or straight, with cresting omitted; the raised panel moulds became straight, and either mitred at the corners or connected with short concave quadrants of the same section (usually astragal), on the outer sides of which a carved or turned rosette was often applied. This feature continued until *circa* 1770 (Fig. 117).

About this date, on some fine examples by Robert Adam, the panels, frieze, etc., were finely carved in his classic taste with vases, foliated scrolls and swags, rams'

164

FIG. 118.—AN OAK WARDROBE (*c.* 1760).

A fine example of a country-made piece, possibly from Lancashire. The panels are moulded and splayed in architectural manner; the diversity in their proportion and grouping is most interesting and instructive. The angle posts are widely chamfered, the splay being very much more to the front than the side; they are worked with a slight entasis and have ogee stops. The lower section is fitted with six drawers lined in pine. The cornice is of typical "mahogany" section. The back is enclosed by oak panels. The joints of the framing retain the old use of oak dowel pegs.

Lower carcase : Width, 4 ft. $5\frac{1}{4}$ in. Height. 1 ft. $9\frac{1}{2}$ in. Depth, 1 ft. $5\frac{3}{4}$ in.
Top   ,,   ,,   4 ft. $2\frac{1}{2}$ in.   ,,   4 ft. $5\frac{1}{2}$ in.   ,,   1 ft. $4\frac{1}{2}$ in.

The property of R. Minton Taylor, Esq.

FIG. 119.—A STANDING CORNER CUPBOARD IN
MAHOGANY (c. 1760).

*The carcase is of pine veneered in mahogany. The doors
are in solid wood, with splayed and moulded panels in ovolo
moulded rails and stiles, reflecting the design of contemporary
doors in houses, etc. The moulded cornice has a dentil course,
and the flat frieze is bordered with bands of inlay. The
bracket feet are of cabriole section.*

Height, 4 ft. 6½ in.   Width, 2 ft. 11 in.

The property of Stanley J. May, Esq.

heads, the honeysuckle, and other motifs in low relief. Inlay in contrasting colours, in which the Adam influence was dominant, was also beginning to enliven the panels, this being carried on by Hepplewhite, Sheraton, and numerous contemporary cabinet-makers.

Wardrobes of average quality made during the last quarter of the eighteenth century were mostly of " batchelor " type, in two parts. The top half had sides of solid Honduras mahogany, dovetailed to the top and bottom of pine: the panelled pine back was screwed into rebates.

The cornice was generally a separate unit, framed in pine and faced with mahogany mouldings, with, in some cases, a cross-banded veneered frieze.

The pair of doors were often framed and panelled in Cuba wood, the panels being veneered on the outer face with curl figure and surrounded by a tiny moulding in the rebate.

To cover the joint between the meeting stiles an astragal moulded* brass strip was screwed to the locking door. The interior was fitted with sliding oak trays.

The bottom half was generally constructed in pine, veneered straight grain mahogany at the sides, and with curl on the front: the drawers (usually four) having oak linings and mahogany cock beading around the edges.

Around the top edge a moulding was fixed to hide the junction with the top half of the wardrobe. The base was either a moulded plinth with bracket feet or the " swept " foot of French type. In early nineteenth-century specimens, squat turned stumps supported the wardrobe, which considerably impoverished the design.

Eighteenth-century wardrobes in oak of purely country design and construction are very pleasing, and stand in a class by themselves (Fig. 118).

* Usually a reeded strip after 1800.

X.—CORNER CUPBOARDS

CUPBOARDS to stand or to hang in the angles of rooms were popular throughout the eighteenth century, made in oak, walnut, and mahogany, and a large number of interesting specimens exist. They were made either with a flat front and short returns to abut on the walls at right angles (Fig. 119), or were bow-fronted.

The standing cupboards were in one or two sections; in the latter case, both parts were fitted with doors, the upper one sometimes glazed as a show cabinet for china and glass.

Those designed as a small single cupboard with solid panelled door obtained a large amount of support on the dado moulding which was invariably fitted around the old rooms, and in addition nails or screws were driven through the back boards into the plaster or wall panelling.

The interiors were fitted with shelves having a shaped front edge, and often grooved close to the back edges to support plates; the back boards were generally painted a dull green on the inside. During the last quarter of the century both the oak and mahogany specimens were often inlaid with borders, scrolls, the shell, pateræ, etc., and many were fitted with small drawers immediately beneath or inside the cupboard.

The cornices were of similar type to those found on contemporary cabinets, and when on the bow front were built up of narrow sections to obviate end grain coming to the face near the sides; when flat-fronted they were sometimes pedimented, and in very rare cases in the bow front also, but it was an unsuitable treatment in the latter type.

166

XI.—WASHSTANDS

AMONG the bedroom appointments made in mahogany were various types of washstands of very pleasing design, if somewhat inefficient for the purposes of ablution. An early type was a small stand composed of three or four uprights, shaped and turned, and connected at the top by a circular moulded rim for a small bowl; half-way down the legs were framed in with a square or triangular drawer, upon which stood a spherical powder box. At the base a triangular or square block was supported by three or four spreading feet of cabriole form. This type was in use until the middle of the eighteenth century.

The next washstands to appear were variations of a small cabinet upon legs with top and front hinged to open, the interior being fitted, including a sliding mirror at the back.

A simple and well-known type, from *circa* 1770, was the bow-fronted corner washstand, supported upon three rectangular legs, the top holed centrally for a basin and at each side for turned wooden cups. The back was formed of two boards of shaped outline meeting in the angle. Beneath the top a cupboard with a pair of doors was arranged, or instead, and more usually, a shelf connected the legs half-way down with a shallow drawer fitted beneath; also, to tie in the slender legs a second shelf with concave edges was fitted a few inches above the floor. Inlay provided the decoration on fine veneered specimens. Many were made of pine, finished and decorated with painting or gilding; they seldom can be dated prior to 1785.

167

XII.—MIRRORS

1. **WALL MIRRORS.**— The large amount of furniture designed by architects, or under their influence, during the early mahogany period (1715–1745) included many important mirrors to be used as pier glasses. They provided an opportunity perhaps even greater than most articles of furniture for truly architectural treatment, and were cleverly handled by Kent and his contemporaries.

The usual theme was a tall, oblong, bevelled plate (sometimes in two pieces) framed in a broad, moulded, and carved architrave, surmounted with classic frieze and cornice, with broken pediment and central finial such as a cartouche; the architrave terminated in base scrolls and rested upon a surbase mould, beneath which a shaped apron piece was fixed, ornamented with carving.

They were chiefly of pinewood, gilt; others were faced with mahogany or walnut with enriched mouldings and carving picked out in gilt). Gesso also played an important part in decorating the gilt specimens, and was still popular as the chief means of working the enrichment on the less important mirror frames (Fig. 120).

A contemporary mirror of quite different arrangement was a long, low glass to stand on the mantelshelf, known as a landscape mirror. The frame was about $1\frac{1}{2}$ or 2 inches wide in walnut, lacquer, or gilt gesso. Those with cross-banded mouldings are often dated prior to 1720. In certain cases the short sides were enriched with projecting scroll-pieces carved with acanthus. The mirror was arranged in three bevelled plates—a long centre glass with a narrow plate on each side, the former just clipping the side bevels of the latter.

168

FIG. 120.—AN EARLY GEORGIAN WALL MIRROR
(*c*. 1725).

The frame is of deal with pediment, cartouche, scrolls, and central shell carved in deal ; the whole surface is covered in gesso composition, in which is worked the ornament in low relief, and finished in gilt. The mirror plate has a flat bevel which follows the inward point at the top corners.

N.B.—The cartouche form is a corruption of the spread eagle.

Width, 1 ft. 11 in.   Height, 3 ft. 3 in.

The property of Stanley J. May, Esq.

FIG. 121.—A WALL MIRROR IN CARVED GILT FRAME (*c.* 1745).

The design is typical of the rococo style but is an early specimen, and consequently is more reserved and orderly in treatment than many produced after 1750.

Candle sconces are fitted to the lower part.

FIG. 122.—A MAHOGANY-FRAMED MIRROR
(*c*. 1750).

The narrow frame is moulded and mitred, the inner member being carved and gilt. The two top corners have the typical inward point. The fret-cut cresting and baseboards are veneered in mahogany. The usual bird carved in relief and gilded occupies the central position on the former.

Height, 3 ft.   Width, 1 ft. 7 in.

The property of Stanley J. May, Esq.

FIG. 123.—A MAHOGANY TOILET MIRROR
(c. 1745).

The mirror frame is similar to that used in wall mirrors (see Fig. 122). The supports are straight with turned mahogany finials. The box stand is veneered on pine and fitted with three small drawers, the front being of hollow section. A small plinth with bracket feet form the supports.

Height, 2 ft. 3 in.   Width, 1 ft. 3½ in.

The property of Stanley J. May, Esq.

About 1745 the wall mirrors became lighter and very free in design, responding to the French Messonnier style (Fig. 121); this induced the intensely rococo forms, in which from *circa* 1750 frames were carved in a restless " arrangement " of undercut scrolls and leafage more suggestive of metal than carved wood. On such mirrors the bevelled edge no longer obtained. They remained popular until *circa* 1765, and were made by Chippendale and many contemporary craftsmen. When Robert Adam began designing wall mirrors (and many of his original drawings for these still exist), he insisted on simple geometrical forms in composing the main lines, adding enrichment more reservedly in his own inimitable style. For mantel glasses a horizontal ellipse was a favourite early shape, surrounded by grouped C scrolls carved in the Chippendale manner; his later and more classic glasses were often composed of three or more mirrors in rectangular framing, with ornament (much of it over the glass) composed of vases, pateræ, medallions, festoons, scrolls, bows of ribbon, and pendent husks, of which a good deal was moulded in a special composition upon wire cores, finished gilt.

A type of mahogany framed mirror became very popular *circa* 1750 for the smaller houses, composed on the lines of the narrow walnut frames, usually a tall rectangle with a small inward point at the two top corners, to which the bevelled edge of the plate was made to correspond; there was a projecting flat outer frame, or surround, narrow at the sides, but widening at the top and base, with intricate fret-cut edges. The top cresting was generally enriched with a gilt bird, carved in relief in a pierced circle (Fig. 122). The edge of the frame against the glass also had a gilt fillet.

A late eighteenth-century favourite was the convex mirror in a moulded circular frame gilt, the outer edge reeded and banded at intervals with cross-ribbons, and with a black reeded fillet next the glass; in the hollow of the moulding small gilt balls were applied at intervals.

169

Such mirrors were often surmounted by an eagle with outspread wings and carved foliage.

Contemporary with the circular convex mirror from *circa* 1790 was a type of rectangular overmantel glass, designed usually with bevelled central and two side plates, surrounded and separated by a narrow reeded frame; a bold pilaster stood at each side, the whole being crowned with a curious hollow moulded cornice in which the row of balls also appears; square bosses were generally arranged at the junctions of the framing, faced with pateræ; feet were provided of spherical form. The enrichment of the mouldings and carving is generally of " Empire " character; they were popular throughout the first third of the nineteenth century, and to the end of it in country districts.

2. TOILET MIRRORS.—The very charming little mirrors mounted upon box stands containing drawers, of the type described and illustrated in Part II., continued in favour for many years in company with the other bedroom appointments in walnut wood. Prior to 1735–1740 mahogany toilet mirrors were a great rarity, and were none too common before 1750. The early models were designed with a rectangular mirror in a narrow moulded frame, having an inward point at the two top corners and an inner carved fillet, gilt; this was suspended by brass screw mirror movements on square tapered uprights, usually moulded and fitted with turned finials. The base was a shallow veneered box containing one row of small drawers, and was supported on bracket feet under a small plinth mould. The faces of the drawers and framing were shaped concave in section, with a small ovolo usually around the top edges (Fig. 123). In many cases a fret-cut cresting was fitted to the mirror head, but is seldom intact to-day. The glass was Vauxhall plate with flat wide bevel.

With the established influence of Robert Adam and his followers the form of some chair backs provided excellent shapes for small mirrors, the most interesting specimens

FIG. 124.—A SHIELD-SHAPE TOILET MIRROR
(*c.* 1780).

The mirror frame is faced with cross-banded mahogany. The box stand is serpentine in front, and fitted with three drawers ; it is veneered on pine. The drawer linings are of very thin oak. The edges of the box and also of the drawer fronts are inlaid with a rope pattern in boxwood and ebony. The bracket feet are of cabriole form. The drawer knobs and the three urn finials are of turned ivory.

Height, 2 ft. 2 in.   Width, 1 ft. 5 in.

The property of Stanley J. May, Esq.

being shield, or oval (actually a beautifully proportioned ellipse). To fit to the shaped sides of these mirrors, the slender uprights were also curved with a little extra playfulness at the lower end. The stand again contained a row of tiny drawers, but with vertical front, though often bowed or serpentine. The mirror frame was now very narrow, quite flat, and cross-banded, the shield shape being built up of sections of pine, and the oval was constructed by wrapping a narrow strip of yew or other easily bendable wood around a former until the desired width was obtained. The box and drawer faces were veneered, and in many cases the mirror supports also. Arris lines and borders of lighter woods and ebony were applied, ivory or bone being used for urn finials or rosettes on the uprights, and as pulls and escutcheons on the drawers. The carcase or box of the stand was invariably framed in pine, the drawer linings being of very thin oak or mahogany (Fig. 124). Mirrors of this type were also faced with satinwood.

The box stand with drawers was omitted in many cases; such were known as cheval glasses, the oval mirror being also arranged with major axis horizontal and suspended in a frame consisting of the usual uprights, framed into trestle feet, and connected by a shaped stretcher. On this framing a border line was incised, or a holly line inlaid.

The less expensive mirrors had rectangular frames, and this form became popular from about 1800, when the uprights (and stretchers when no stand was fitted) were turned in very refined and delicate profiles. The face of the mirror frame was still cross-banded, but frequently of convex section. The mirror movements were often faced with turned knobs (Fig. 111).

XIII.—LACQUER

In Part II. (p. 93) I gave a brief account of lacquered furniture of the walnut period, and the manner in which the process was applied in England.

Between 1715 and 1725, when mahogany was gaining favour, the demand for lacquered furniture was still comparatively great, but it had largely declined by 1735, when fashion demanded the architectural and heavy style of Kent, either entirely gilt or in carved mahogany.

The craze for lacquer, however, revived with the lighter style of the ensuing period, and decidedly came into its own with the Chinese taste, *circa* 1755. Probably the most fashionable piece was the lacquered cabinet upon a stand, the latter being of side-table form, but richly carved on the legs and frieze and entirely gilt; those stands more simply decorated were often finished in lacquer.

Until *circa* 1745 the Carolean style cabinet remained, fitted with a pair of richly decorated doors, secured by several elaborately cut and shaped brass hinge - plates, with corresponding lock-plates; there was no cornice (Fig. 125). Between 1740 and 1750 the cabinets became taller, and were designed with cornices. The stands became more restrained, though they retained the enriched cabriole leg. The brass work gradually lost its important position in the scheme, and by *circa* 1760 it consisted merely of a small key escutcheon and plain brass butts hidden in the joints of the doors. By this date the legs were square.

Lacquer decoration was also applied to bookcases, bureaux, beds, chests of drawers, mirrors, chairs, clocks, etc. It was sparingly used by Robert Adam. It also appeared on tables, chairs, cabinets, etc., in the Hepplewhite and Sheraton styles, but the art had largely degenerated to painting by 1780.

172

FIG. 125.—AN ENGLISH LACQUER CABINET, FITTED WITH
DRAWERS, UPON A LACQUER STAND (*c.* 1730).

*The cabinet is of the simple rectangular form without cornice, the
ornate hinges and lock-plate being prominent features of the design.*

*The stand has the fashionable hollow frieze ; the cabriole legs are
much enriched and connected by fantastic carved scrolls to the central
cartouche which bears a female head.*

FIG. 126.—A LONG-CASE CLOCK DATING FROM THE
MIDDLE OF THE EIGHTEENTH CENTURY.

*The dial is inscribed " Josh Crosshill, N. Walsham."
The case is of oak veneered in curl mahogany of fine
quality. The finials are of turned wood gilt.*

Height, 7 ft. 8 in.

The property of Stanley J. May, Esq.

XIV.—CLOCKS

LONG-CASE clocks in mahogany are very rare prior to the middle of the eighteenth century, and this may be due to the growing demand for bracket clocks, of which many beautiful specimens were made between 1715 and 1750.

When, therefore, the long case was revived, there was little influence or tradition remaining of the walnut designs. The grace of tall and slender proportions which characterized the clocks of William III. and Anne's reigns was unfortunately seldom repeated; the mahogany cases were wider, the body not so long, and usually the base was somewhat squat. The hood was arched and surmounted by shaped crestings or pediment with finials.

The hood door will be found hinged on a pair of projecting butts, so that it opens within the angle columns, the latter being permanently fixed. The body door was now headed by a shouldered arch, and prior to *circa* 1760 a raised panel was generally placed on the base (Fig. 126, and see diagrams, p. 97).

The carcase was of oak, mahogany, or pine, veneered with figured mahogany or lacquered.

Fine specimens in mahogany had applied frets on splayed corners and on the frieze of the cornice. Carving was also present on the hood, the case door, and the plinth, and inlay in the late specimens.

A large number of country clock cases were made during the second half of the eighteenth century in simple oak forms, at times inlaid on the solid and generally with painted iron dials; a number of them were only thirty-hour clocks, and for cheapness retained the straight cornice with square head to dial and case door as in the walnut fashion.

173

XV.—BEDS

THE enormous height given to beds during the reigns of William III. and Anne continued under George I. for a few years; but the growing popularity of mahogany and its fine qualities soon induced important alterations. These firstly concerned the materials with which the posts and cornices had been covered; they were now being dispensed with, also the height of the posts was considerably reduced. The cornices of mahogany beds were smaller in scale, and rapidly discarded the fantastic shapes in the gilded and carved cresting; they resembled, in fact, the classic type applied to important cabinets, and were entirely exposed. The posts at the foot, also exposed, were turned and delicately carved in low relief above the level of the mattress; at the base they terminated in short cabriole legs, but about 1750 these were generally omitted, and a small plinth was added to the square post. The head posts were plain square tapered, intended to be hidden by curtains; generally they were in a native hard wood.

During the periods of Gothic and Chinese taste important beds were decorated accordingly, and fitted with remarkable hoods resembling pagoda roofs; the Chinese lattice was also fitted at the head between the posts (see the Chinese lacquer bed at Victoria and Albert Museum).

About 1760 the foot posts became still more delicate, and were generally fluted on the taper above a vase form. In some instances low relief carving appeared in sunk panels on the square lower portions of the foot posts, which now began to taper to a spade plinth.

Robert Adam designed some remarkable state beds,

174

FIG. 127.—A MAHOGANY FOUR-POST BEDSTEAD (*c.* 1765).

The foot posts turned, fluted and carved. The moulded cornice shaped in serpentine curves.

Width, 5 ft. 2 in.   Length, 7 ft.   Height, 8 ft.

The property of Messrs. Phillips, of Hitchin.

in which satinwood and gilding were employed, and also many of simple structure in mahogany with beautiful low relief carving on the posts and cornice.

From about 1765 the so-called Hepplewhite beds appeared; they were marked by their graceful proportions and refinement of detail; the posts were turned, reeded, and carved with palm leaf and wheat-ear. The cornice was frequently bowed or serpentine, carved, pierced, and inlaid. Painted decoration is to be found on some from about 1780, taking the place of carving.

In the last decade of the eighteenth century, decadence in the design of four-posters becomes apparent; particularly is this noticeable in the hitherto finely executed foot posts, which now began to lose their beautiful proportions, and, although but little increased in diameter, the ornament appears somewhat coarse; this tendency increased after 1800, the designs getting heavy and very ugly in comparison with the superb models of twenty years earlier.

In the eighteenth and early nineteenth century beds the side and end beams were tenoned into the four posts, and secured with coach screws. A series of wooden laths replaced the earlier roped-on canvas mattress.

The turning of the long posts was an expensive and difficult undertaking on the lathe of the eighteenth century, and although it is usually impossible to detect the joint, many posts were built up of two parts, and united by a strong dowel; this economized material and enabled the turning to be done on a normal size lathe, as only the best-equipped workshops could boast of a lathe capable of receiving a post about 8 feet long.

XVI.—FIRE SCREENS

THE fire screens of the early mahogany period followed the lines of fine examples in Queen Anne walnut. They consisted of a low rectangular panel with shaped top, surmounted by a carved cresting. A needlework picture filled the panel. The side posts carried down to trestle feet, which were connected by turned and carved stretchers. From the second quarter of the century this type was made with a sliding panel in an outer frame.

The pole screen became popular about 1740, though fine specimens exist which bear all the characteristics of the first years of mahogany. They consisted of a small tripod foot, similar to the small circular-top tables, upon which was fixed a short turned stem supporting a slender pole. On this pole a panel was arranged to slide, and to be secured at any height by means of a spring or screw. The panel frame was at first rectangular, and often carved with the flower and ribbon (Fig. 128). From about 1760 the panels assumed the shapes of contemporary chairs— *e.g.*, the shield, oval, and rectangle; needlework continued to be the favourite material for display, and largely contributed to their delightful effect. Late examples often had a solid turned or shaped base instead of the tripod foot.

(a)   (b)

FIG. 128.—TWO MAHOGANY POLE SCREENS: (a) c. 1730,
(b) 1760.

The tripod feet are in form similar to those used for many tea
tables. The pole is secured in the stem which is finely turned, and
carved with spiral fluting in (b). The needlework panel is framed
in mahogany.

The property of Frank Partridge, Esq.

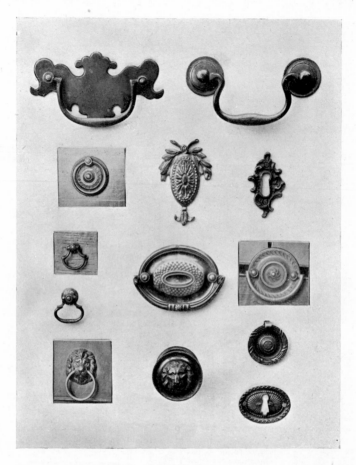

FIG. 129.—BRASS MOUNTS OF THE EIGHTEENTH CENTURY.

The solid and the pierced back-plates were in use on late walnut and on mahogany until c. 1750, but the simple loop on two circular roses had come in about c. 1735–40.

The second row shows cast and enriched brass mounts in use c. 1760–80.

The third row shows an oval and a circular back-plate of stamped brass with cast loops as introduced after 1788.

The lion-head knob and the cast head with ring date from c. 1790.

DRAWER CONSTRUCTION.

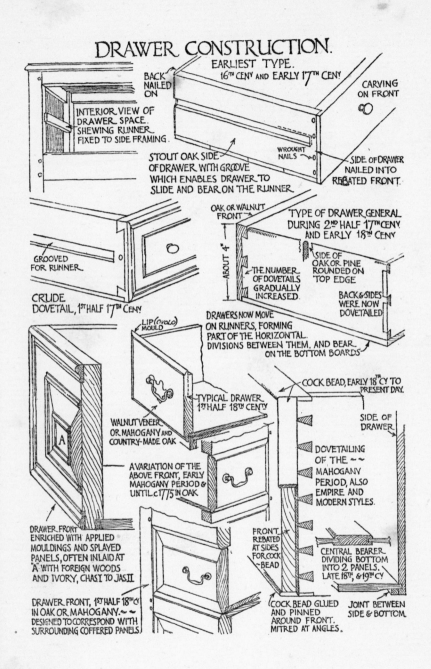

EARLIEST TYPE.
16TH CENY AND EARLY 17TH CENY

BACK NAILED ON

CARVING ON FRONT

INTERIOR VIEW OF DRAWER SPACE. SHEWING RUNNER FIXED TO SIDE FRAMING.

STOUT OAK SIDE OF DRAWER WITH GROOVE WHICH ENABLES DRAWER TO SLIDE AND BEAR ON THE RUNNER

WROUGHT NAILS

SIDE OF DRAWER NAILED INTO REBATED FRONT.

GROOVED FOR RUNNER

OAK OR WALNUT FRONT

ABOUT 4"

TYPE OF DRAWER GENERAL DURING 2ND HALF 17TH CENY. AND EARLY 18TH CENY

THE NUMBER OF DOVETAILS GRADUALLY INCREASED.

SIDE OF OAK OR PINE ROUNDED ON TOP EDGE

BACK & SIDES WERE NOW DOVETAILED

CRUDE DOVETAIL, 1ST HALF 17TH CENY.

DRAWERS NOW MOVE ON RUNNERS, FORMING PART OF THE HORIZONTAL DIVISIONS BETWEEN THEM, AND BEAR ON THE BOTTOM BOARDS

LIP (OVOLO) MOULD

TYPICAL DRAWER 1ST HALF 18TH CENY

WALNUT VENEER OR MAHOGANY AND COUNTRY-MADE OAK

A VARIATION OF THE ABOVE FRONT, EARLY MAHOGANY PERIOD & UNTIL c1775 IN OAK

A

DRAWER FRONT ENRICHED WITH APPLIED MOULDINGS AND SPLAYED PANELS, OFTEN INLAID AT 'A' WITH FOREIGN WOODS AND IVORY, CHAS I TO JAS II

DRAWER FRONT, 1ST HALF 18TH CY IN OAK OR MAHOGANY. DESIGNED TO CORRESPOND WITH SURROUNDING COFFERED PANELS.

COCK BEAD, EARLY 18TH CY TO PRESENT DAY.

SIDE OF DRAWER

DOVETAILING OF THE MAHOGANY PERIOD, ALSO EMPIRE AND MODERN STYLES.

FRONT REBATED AT SIDES FOR COCK BEAD

CENTRAL BEARER DIVIDING BOTTOM INTO 2 PANELS. LATE 18TH & 19TH CY

COCK BEAD GLUED AND PINNED AROUND FRONT. MITRED AT ANGLES.

JOINT BETWEEN SIDE & BOTTOM.

M

CHAIRS: DEVELOPMENT of STRETCHERS & SEAT FRAMING.
16TH & 17TH CENTURY EXAMPLES.

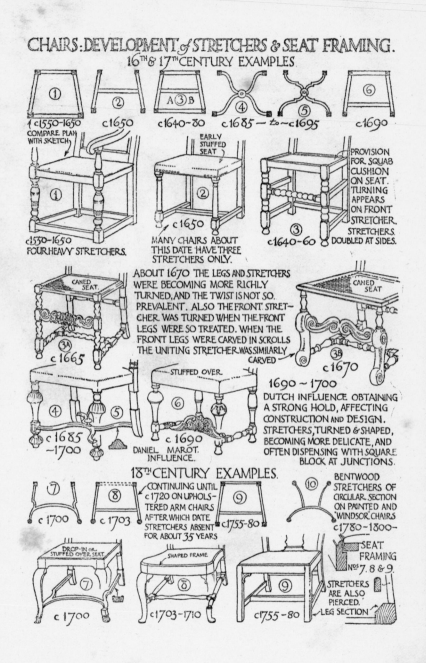

① c1550-1650
COMPARE PLAN WITH SKETCH

② c1650

A ③ B

④ c1685 — to — c1695

⑤

⑥ c1690

① c1550-1650 FOUR HEAVY STRETCHERS.

② c1650 MANY CHAIRS ABOUT THIS DATE HAVE THREE STRETCHERS ONLY.
EARLY STUFFED SEAT

③ c1640-60
PROVISION FOR SQUAB CUSHION ON SEAT. TURNING APPEARS ON FRONT STRETCHER. STRETCHERS DOUBLED AT SIDES.

③A c1665
CANED SEAT.

ABOUT 1670 THE LEGS AND STRETCHERS WERE BECOMING MORE RICHLY TURNED, AND THE TWIST IS NOT SO PREVALENT. ALSO THE FRONT STRETCHER WAS TURNED WHEN THE FRONT LEGS WERE SO TREATED. WHEN THE FRONT LEGS WERE CARVED IN SCROLLS THE UNITING STRETCHER WAS SIMILARLY CARVED

③B c1670
CANED SEAT

④⑤ c1685-1700

⑥ c1690
STUFFED OVER.
DANIEL MAROT. INFLUENCE.

1690 ~ 1700
DUTCH INFLUENCE OBTAINING A STRONG HOLD, AFFECTING CONSTRUCTION AND DESIGN. STRETCHERS, TURNED & SHAPED, BECOMING MORE DELICATE, AND OFTEN DISPENSING WITH SQUARE BLOCK AT JUNCTIONS.

18TH CENTURY EXAMPLES.

⑦ c1700

⑧ c1703

CONTINUING UNTIL c1720 ON UPHOLSTERED ARM CHAIRS AFTER WHICH DATE STRETCHERS ABSENT FOR ABOUT 35 YEARS

⑨ c1755-80

⑩
BENTWOOD STRETCHERS OF CIRCULAR SECTION ON PAINTED AND WINDSOR CHAIRS c1780-1800~

⑦ c1700
DROP-IN or STUFFED OVER SEAT.

⑧ c1703-1710
SHAPED FRAME.

⑨ c1755-80

SEAT FRAMING Nos 7. 8 & 9.
STRETCHERS ARE ALSO PIERCED.
LEG SECTION

178

EXAMPLES of CORNICE PROFILES, 17TH & 18TH C^{ES}

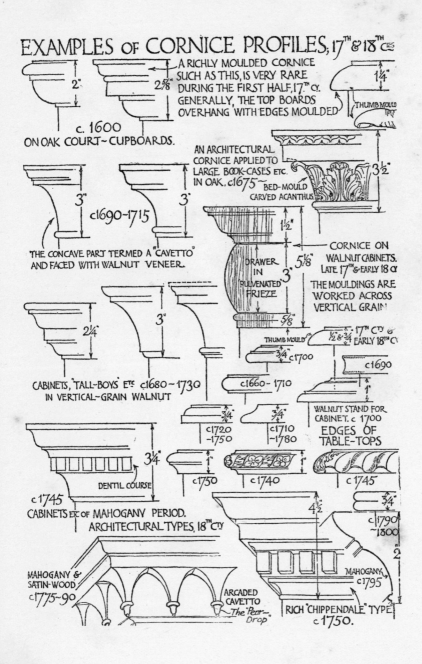

2"

c. 1600
ON OAK COURT~CUPBOARDS.

2⅝"

A RICHLY MOULDED CORNICE
SUCH AS THIS, IS VERY RARE
DURING THE FIRST HALF, 17TH CY.
GENERALLY, THE TOP BOARDS
OVERHANG WITH EDGES MOULDED

1¼"

THUMB MOULD

AN ARCHITECTURAL
CORNICE APPLIED TO
LARGE BOOK-CASES ETC.
IN OAK. c1675 BED-MOULD
CARVED ACANTHUS

3½"

3"   3"
c1690~1715

THE CONCAVE PART TERMED A "CAVETTO"
AND FACED WITH WALNUT VENEER.

1½"

DRAWER
IN
PULVENATED
FRIEZE

5⅛"

3"

5⅛"

CORNICE ON
WALNUT CABINETS.
LATE 17TH & EARLY 18 C^I

THE MOULDINGS ARE
WORKED ACROSS
VERTICAL GRAIN

2¼"   3"

CABINETS, "TALL-BOYS" E^{TC} c1680~1730
IN VERTICAL-GRAIN WALNUT

THUMB MOULD
¾" c1700

c1660~1710

½ & ¾
½   17TH C^{TY} &
EARLY 18TH C^I

c1690

1"

¾"   ¾"
c1720   c1710
~1750   ~1780

WALNUT STAND FOR
CABINET. c1700
EDGES OF
TABLE-TOPS

3¾"

DENTIL COURSE

1"   1"
c1750   c1740   c1745

c1745
CABINETS E^{TC} OF MAHOGANY PERIOD.
ARCHITECTURAL TYPES, 18TH C^{TY}

4½"

¾"
c1790
~1800

2"

MAHOGANY &
SATIN-WOOD
c1775~90

ARCADED
CAVETTO
~The "Pear-
Drop"

MAHOGANY
c1795

RICH "CHIPPENDALE" TYPE
c1750.

179

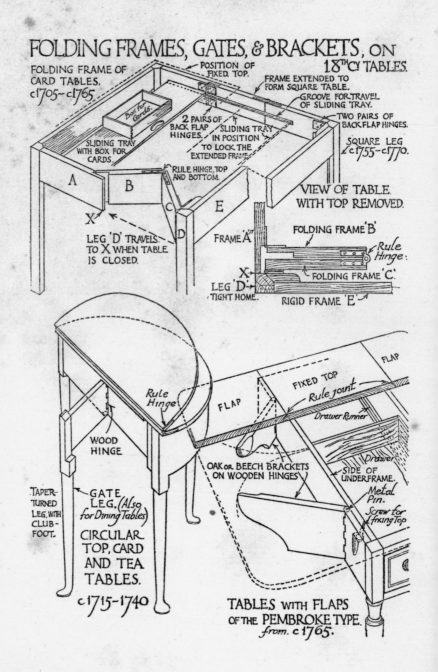

FOLDING FRAMES, GATES, & BRACKETS, ON 18TH CY TABLES.

FOLDING FRAME OF CARD TABLES. c1705~c1765

POSITION OF FIXED TOP.

FRAME EXTENDED TO FORM SQUARE TABLE.

GROOVE FOR TRAVEL OF SLIDING TRAY.

Box for Cards.

2 PAIRS OF BACK FLAP HINGES.

SLIDING TRAY IN POSITION TO LOCK THE EXTENDED FRAME.

TWO PAIRS OF BACK FLAP HINGES.

SQUARE LEG c1755-c1770.

SLIDING TRAY WITH BOX FOR CARDS.

RULE HINGE, TOP AND BOTTOM.

A

B

C

E

D

X

LEG 'D' TRAVELS TO X WHEN TABLE IS CLOSED.

FRAME 'A'

VIEW OF TABLE, WITH TOP REMOVED.

FOLDING FRAME 'B'

Rule Hinge.

FOLDING FRAME 'C'

X

LEG 'D' TIGHT HOME.

RIGID FRAME 'E'

Rule Hinge

WOOD HINGE.

FLAP

FIXED TOP

Rule joint

Drawer Runner

FLAP

Drawer

SIDE OF UNDERFRAME.

OAK OR BEECH BRACKETS ON WOODEN HINGES

Metal Pin.

Screw for fixing Top

TAPER-TURNED LEG, WITH CLUB-FOOT.

GATE LEG. (Also for Dining Tables)

CIRCULAR TOP, CARD AND TEA TABLES. c1715-1740

TABLES WITH FLAPS OF THE PEMBROKE TYPE. from c1765.

180

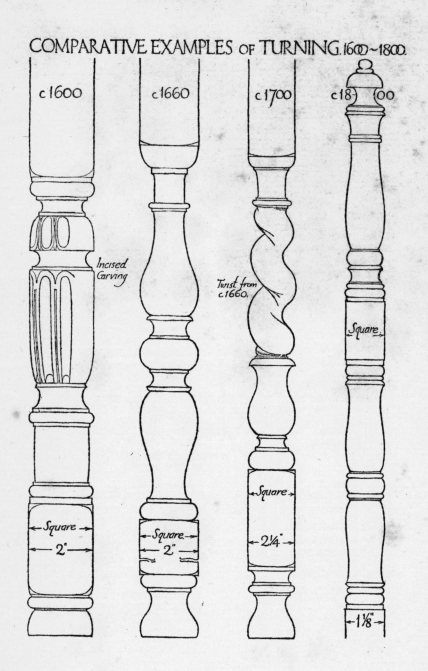

COMPARATIVE EXAMPLES OF TURNING. 1600~1800.

c 1600

c 1660

c 1700

c 18 00

Incised Carving

Twist from c 1660.

Square

Square 2"

Square 2"

Square 2¼"

1⅛"

181

APPENDIX

THE COLLECTOR'S TIME TABLE.

Article or Feature.	Approximate Year of Introduction.	Approximate Year of Cessation.	Remarks.
BUREAU:			
With slant flap	c. 1700	c. 1790	Largely superseded by drawer front and cylinder types after 1775.
With falling drawer front	c. 1765	c. 1820	Ceased during " Sheraton" decline.
With cylinder slide	c. 1785	—	Used almost exclusively after 1800, and continued to modern work.
CHESTS OF DRAWERS:			
1. Straight front, in oak	c. 1600	c. 1700	In late Elizabethan and Jacobean styles. Also country work in all styles.
Straight front, in walnut	c. 1680	c. 1735	Veneered on oak or deal.
Straight front, in mahogany	c. 1725	—	Solid or veneer. To modern times.
2. Bow front, in mahogany	c. 1730	—	Veneered. To modern times.
3. Serpentine, in mahogany	c. 1740	c. 1800	Veneered.
1, 2, and 3 in satinwood	c. 1770	c. 1800	Veneered. Rare.
CABRIOLE LEGS:			
With hoof foot	c. 1695	c. 1720	The " pied de biche."
With club foot	c. 1700	c. 1770	The most common form.
With claw and ball foot	c. 1710	c. 1760	With acanthus on knee in mahogany.
With shell on knee	c. 1703	c. 1730	A walnut feature.
With mask on knee	c. 1720	c. 1740	Masks of lion's or satyr's heads.
With cabochon and leaf on knee	c. 1735	c. 1750	From the French.
CHAIR SEATS:			
Stuffed over	c. 1645	—	To modern times.
Stuffed on drop-in frame	c. 1700	c. 1770	Superseded by stuffed-over frames.
Rush seat	c. 1685	—	On country chairs to nineteenth century.

THE COLLECTOR'S TIME TABLE—*Continued.*

Article or Feature.	Approxi- mate Year of Intro- duction.	Approxi- mate Year of Cessa- tion.	Remarks.
CHAIR SEATS (*Continued*):			
Caned seat	c. 1660	—	Little used c. 1710-1780.
Frame dipped in front	c. 1770	c. 1800	Called " saddle seat."
Frame dipped at sides	c. 1805	c. 1825	On " Empire " chairs.
CORNICES OF CLASSIC TYPE:			
With unbroken pediment	c. 1675	c. 1760	Angular or curved.
With broken pediment	c. 1715	c. 1800	Angular or curved and swan neck.
Without pediment	c. 1550	—	To modern times.
With pulvenated frieze	{ c. 1685	c. 1730	On walnut cabinets, etc.
	{ c. 1725	c. 1740	On mahogany architect's furniture.
With fret frieze	c. 1715	c. 1760	In walnut and mahogany.
With inlaid frieze	c. 1775	c. 1800	Adam influence.
With fret-cut cresting	c. 1735	c. 1755	A rare feature.
With solid cresting and balustrading	c. 1790	c. 1810	
With arcaded bed-mould	c. 1770	c. 1800	Commonly called " pear-drop."
CLOCKS, LONG-CASE:			
Veneered in walnut	c. 1685	c. 1730	Fine examples inlaid marquetry.
Veneered in mahogany	c. 1720	c. 1830– 1850	Inlaid after c. 1760.
INLAY (AND MARQUETRY):			
Cut into the solid	c. 1560	c. 1650	On oak and walnut pieces. In country work c. 1775-1800.
In veneer	c. 1680	c. 1730	Marquetry designs on walnut.
In veneer	c. 1760	c. 1820	Classic type originated by Adam. Continued to c. 1820.
Fan in oval and semicircle	c. 1765	c. 1790	Was frequently shaded.
Shell in oval	c. 1780	c. 1805	Was frequently shaded.

THE COLLECTOR'S TIME TABLE—*Continued.*

Article or Feature.	Approximate Year of Introduction.	Approximate Year of Cessation.	Remarks.
LACQUER:	c. 1660	c. 1800	A few pieces imported prior to the Restoration. Declined in favour at certain periods.
MIRRORS:			
In walnut veneered frames	c. 1675	c. 1730	Also in ebony, lacquer, and tortoiseshell.
For toilet, on stand, with drawers	c. 1703	c. 1730	In walnut. Swing mirror.
For toilet, on stand, with drawers	c. 1720	—	In mahogany. To modern times.
For toilet, on stand, cheval form (no drawers in stand)	c. 1730	c. 1800	Oval and shield shape. Square, continued to modern times.
Frames ornamented in gesso gilt	c. 1700	c. 1735	Classical shapes, patterns in low relief.
Frames carved and gilt	c. 1700	—	Rococo style from c. 1745 to 1760.
Large cheval glass	c. 1780	—	To modern times.
Circular convex wall glass	c. 1785	c. 1830	Gilt frame with black slip.
MOULDINGS:			
Worked *with* the grain on the solid	—	—	Throughout all historic periods.
Worked *with* the grain and applied	c. 1625	—	Not employed on veneered walnut pieces.
Worked *across* the grain	c. 1675	c. 1730	On veneered walnut pieces.
Carved mouldings	—	—	Much employed in Gothic, Tudor, and Jacobean periods. Absent in fashionable work c. 1675-1715. Again used on mahogany mouldings from c. 1715.
PAINTED FURNITURE:			
On mediæval oak	—	c. 1575	Chiefly in tempera.
On satinwood and pine	c. 1770	c. 1820	

INDEX

INDEX

PRINTED IN GREAT BRITAIN BY BILLING AND SONS, LTD., GUILDFORD AND ESHER.